THE STATE THEORY OF MONEY: The Lost Chapter

Translated by Marco Saba

November 2018

This text is the only existing English translation from German of the forgotten fourth chapter of the Georg Friedrich Knaap's book **"The State Theory of Money"** (1906) from which much of the so-called MMT was derived. The first three chapter translation can be downloaded from: https://socialsciences.mcmaster.ca/econ/ugcm/3ll3/knapp/StateTheoryMoney.pdf

The original German edition can be found here:

https://archive.org/details/staatlichetheori00knap_0/page/n5

[A quote from the Austria chapter: *"Almost at the moment when the new banking constitution, which had hitherto only actually practiced course regulation, became a legal institution, it repeated itself what had happened in 1859 and 1866: the outbreak of war shook the newly-founded work and completely destroyed it."*]

The 'Lost-in-translation' Fourth Chapter and appendixes from the original "Staatliche Theorie des Geldes"

(pages 303 to 486)

INDEX

Overview by States.

§ 16. England page 6

Brief overview of the English monetary system, from the Middle Ages to 1816.

§17. France page 22

Overview of the French monetary system from 1803 to 1870.

The end of French bimetallism in 1876 by discontinuing the unrestricted silver stamp.

§ 18a. German Empire in 1905 page 41

Description of the former monetary constitution; seven types of money: 1. gold coins; 2. the Reichs silver coins; 3. the Nickel and copper coins; 4. the thalers; 5. the Reichskasse notes; 6. the notes of the Reichsbank; 7. the marks of some privileged banks.

§ 18b. German Empire; Transition from 1871 to 1876 page 53

Description of the measures by which the gold currency occurred in place of the previous silver currency. - Alleged reasons for the change. The real reason lies in the Inter-party relations with England as the then predominant commercial power.

§ 18c. German Empire; Cover of the Note Issue, 1907 page 69
(from Bankarchiv for 1907)

Sometimes the discount and Lombard rates are increased to secure the so-called third-party coverage of the notes issued by the Reichsbank. Gold in bars, as well as cash in our sense (Reich gold coins) would be the best cover; In addition, however, other types of money are conspicuously permitted as cover funds. Apart from these, there is a lack of clarity about how the bank gets gold, because it should be prepared to redeem other types of gold in gold, while it has no power to force deposits to their coffers in gold money. The gold supply thus depends on the behavior of the customers, which is quite uncertain. Only in quiet times, the customer pays gold coins; In troubled times, he chooses other types of money. The third-party cover is therefore in constant danger.

§ 18d. German Reich from 1905 to 1914   page 78

The disappearance of the thaler. The Reichsbank notes are provided with acceptance obligation. The Laws of 4 August 1914: The treasury note of the German Reich also receive compulsory acceptance. The redemption of the Reichsbank notes. The redemption of the Reichsbank notes and treasury note of the German Reich stops. Loan cash vouchers are created.

Schematic overview of money types for the time after the outbreak of the war.

§ 19a. Austria 1857-1892   page 89

The "Austrian currency", originally a silver currency, introduced because of the inter-group relations with the Zollverein; it is shattered by warlike events, 1859. In 1866 also state notes are created. The silver gulden becomes accessory and receives agio. This agio disappears in June 1878; the silver currency will not be restored, since gold has been introduced in the German Reich.

§ 19b. Austria 1892 to 1900   page 116

It decides transition to the gold standard. First, at pari with the gold money of the Western countries is decided on the basis of the course in the years 1879 to 1891. This purchase of large gold reserves through a gold loan. The bare gold money is created but not put into circulation; the bank will be equipped with gold money. For the time being, the intervalutary agio of German money is by no means disappearing. The exodromic measures begin in 1894 and have the success that the agio of the German currency ceases almost completely. The valutary money of Austria, however, are the banknotes, which remain provisionally insoluble. The two states of the monarchy still promise redemption.

APPENDICES AND ADDITIONS

§ 19c. The customs payment in Austria from 1854 to 1900   page 132

The customs payment is exempt from the "common" law, it is under special law, since 1854. Payment of tariffs in silver from 1854 to 1878; Payment of tariffs in gold from 1878 on. The purpose is to provide the means to pay interest on certain bonds. There were bonds with interest in silver, as long as Germany had silver currency; and those with interest in gold since the German Reich has gold currency. "Guilders in silver" and "Guilders in gold" are special units of value (next to the gulden par excellence), which are used for special business. This separation ceases, however, as soon as the silver coins, respectively the gold coins have no agio.

§ 19d. Austria-Hungary 1901 to 1914   page 146

The state notes have disappeared. Two-crown pieces are created. Schematic overview of the Austro-Hungarian monetary system before the outbreak of the war; Comparison with the German monetary system. Gold service at the Austro-Hungarian bank. Attempts to put the 20 kroner gold pieces "into circulation"; this is not a fundamental, but only occasional voluntary cash payment. There is no question of redeeming the notes in gold. The Customs Gold Ordinance is a cash-redemption of notes limited to customs. More about the regulation of the Inter-valutary courses against the western countries.

§ 20. Understanding about money and prices   page 163

"Value" always requires a comparison. Depending on the object with which you compare the money, there is an expression of the value of the money. These different expressions stand side by side independently, must not be confused, and even less be regarded as one. One can compare the money also with groups of goods; but the composition of the group must be arranged. Index numbers are welcome hints about changes in the price of goods included in the group. Other groups would yield different index numbers. Price changes always take place; they have their reasons in the circumstances of the market; they can not be explained by the assumption that the monetary value has changed in the opposite sense, because that would be a tautology: one only knows something about the value of money through price statistics, and so can not explain it by itself. As regards income, one wonders whether one is a consumer of goods or whether one is a producer: the price changes of the goods are then perceived very differently. The change of prices has no influence on the "validity" of the pieces; therefore, it is important to keep separate the state theory of money and economic considerations on money.

Annexes

- **Literature about the state theory of money**   page 174

- **Postscript of February 26, 1921**   page 190

Chapter Four.

Overview of states.

§ 16. England

The English State forms a numerical community in which, since William the Conqueror, the unit of value has been named "Pound Sterling"; the 20th part is called Schilling; the 240th Part of the pound Sterling is called Pfennig. The recurrent connection of this unit of value took place in this way: the pound sterling is legally equivalent to the weight of silver, which had previously been used in an autometallist manner as unit of value. That's the historical definition of the sterling pound. As a means of payment were introduced by William the Conqueror coins; there were no other means of payment; the coins were made of silver; there was only one kind of coin; they were after the proclamation, that is, they had a constitution or, what is the same thing, they were money. Since the public funds in this - only - make money, so this money was valuta. So there was silver currency, first in the Platonic sense; but also in the genetic Meaning, for it was taken for granted that all silver could be transformed into money by the mint of the king. On the other hand, there was no silver currency in the drastic sense, since there was no provision for only nearly fully important silver money in circulation.

The silver of the fineness 220/240 was called standard silver; it was "hylic" metal; next to it was no other hylic metal. The unit of weight used in the Tower, where the mint was, was the Tower Pound (= 15/16 of the later Troy Pound). Initially, only coins were struck that were proclaimed a penny; they were cash money. Under William the Conqueror, the penny-piece had the value of 1/240 Tower Pound standard silver. Thus, the transition from the autometallist constitution to the monetary constitution was a pending one (pp. 187-188).

The definition of the standard silver is still valid today; also the interdependence of the three terms pound sterling, shilling, penny is still present today. On the other hand, Henry VIII introduced the Troy Pound as a weight unit (which is given as 373.2419 grams); it breaks down into 12 ounces, the ounce into 20 penny weights - and this ounce is still in use today for the silver trade.

Under Henry VII (1485-1509) and especially under Heinrich VIII (1509-1547), larger silver coins appear, the proclaimed to 12 pennies; they are called shilling pieces,

Also under Henry VIII appear silver coins, which are proclaimed to 5 shillings; they are called crowns. Under Mary of the Catholic (1553-1558) pieces are beaten to 2 and 1/2 shillings; they are called half crowns. Pieces proclaimed as 2 shillings also occur: they are called Florin (gulden), but were not written until 1849.

As you know, there never was a silver coin worth one pound sterling.

The content of these larger pieces is always proportional to their validity. This proportionality seems to be self-evident to the metallist; For us it is only a permissible phenomenon, which is based on a special arrangement. It follows that the specific content of the larger pieces is always the same as that of the penny piece of the period in question. But the specific content of the pfennig piece is changeable; it gets smaller and smaller over time. Accordingly, the concept of the penny does not depend on the value; one could say: denarius est quem rex demonstrat.

The specific content of the pfennig piece-if we take the penny as a unit of value-is the reciprocal expression of the coin's foot for the pfennig piece, and the development of this coinage was, according to the excellent work of Lord Liverpool (1805):

Name of the king: Number of pennies hit from one pound of standard silver:

	from the Tower Pound:		from the Troy Pound:
Wilhelm I......................	240		
Edward I (28th year).......	243		
Eduard III. (18th year)....	266		
Eduard III. (20th year)....	270		
Eduard III. (27th year)....	300		
Henry IV (13th year).......	360		
Edward IV (4th year)......	450		
Henry VIII (18th year).....	506 1/2	=	540
Elisabeth (2nd year).........	675	=	720
Elisabeth (43rd year)........	697 1/2	=	744 pieces.

At the latter coin foot one has then held; From then on, Troy Pound standard silver was always applied at 744 pfennigs = 62 shillings, as long as argyrolepsia existed.

Consequently, the Pfennig under Wilhelm I contained 1/240 Tower pound standard silver; however, under Elizabeth (43rd year of her reign) only 1/697.5 Towerpfund standard silver.
From this classic example of medieval "coin deterioration", it follows that the pound sterling in coins originally contained a Tower Pound standard silver; but since the 43rd year of Elisabeth it only contained 240/697.5 Towerpfund standard silver; and all this has no effect on the legal-historical concept of the pound sterling.

Since the royal coffers always paid in the coins of the last coin foot, the coins of the last coin foot are valutary; the coins of the older coin base, if still valid, thus became accessory - but since they received an agio because of their higher specific content, they were withdrawn from circulation. On the other hand, at that time all those coins were cash money: the newest, because their specific value corresponded exactly to the standard to which the silver was fundamentally converted into money without restriction; the older ones, because their specific value - which we correctly present - was not less than that of the norm. Thus, that time knew no emergency (or paratypical) money; the bare (orthotypical) money had sole power.

Furthermore, all money was worth as much as the metal it was made of; there was no depleted money or money with a purely optional anepicentric assumption.

Likewise, all the money was definite; the provisional (redeemable) money had not yet come to light.

The evils that result from the so-called coin deterioration - and the reasons for desolation, which lie in the amphitropical position of the individual, should not be repeated here (see above p. 39).

After the 43rd year of the reign of Queen Elizabeth, the specific content of the coins has not been further reduced. On the other hand, the wear of the coins has always increased and was not combated because the state did not want to bring the necessary sacrifices.

This continual wear has not been without influence on the repeated deliberate reduction of the specific content of the coins, but must be regarded as a special event, since obviously the reduction in the specific content was far greater than the progressive wear. It is also evident that always the newer, lighter pennies had the same validity as the old, heavier pennies; otherwise the reduction of the specific content would be incomprehensible. Just keep in mind that the whole process would make no sense if old and new pennies were allowed to hold their weight.

Then one would have had morphic-pensatory means of payment, and it would be hard to see why the specific content of the pieces was always lowered. It is precisely this reduction that proves that the pieces were meant as a kind of currency, but that technical expression was lacking.

This strict adherence to the bar constitution, despite the changes in the hylogenic norm (which was an argyrogenic norm here), is easily explained: it had not yet been discovered that emergency communication was sufficient for internal traffic. On the other hand, it was clear that the bar constitution offered great advantages for the then little-developed foreign trade; for the bare money had the advantage that at any rate it remained usable in foreign lands; this use thus secured a minimum rate for English money abroad, which depended on how much silver was valued as commodity abroad according to the units of value prevailing there. In the English constitution of the Bar, therefore, there was a certain certainty that English money abroad was somehow to be affixed as a commodity-though by no means certain that it was always the same; it was even lower, due to the reduced specific content (not to mention the wear and tear) - but at least it had to be done, and that was enough.

The constitution of the Bar contained in it a certain crude attempt in the direction of exodromy - that is its true meaning in ancient times, when the idea of an exodromic administration was still quite out of sight.

The other fates of English monetary affairs arise from the appearance of gold coins, especially those gold coins, which received the name Guinea; Charles II. (1660-1685) beat Guineen from 1663; the standard gold used had the fineness 220/240 (while the standard silver had the fineness 222 / 240, so was "finer").

From the Troy Pound standard gold 44 1/2 guineas were beaten; that's the coin foot. Presumably one could then buy the quantity of gold contained in Guinea for one pound sterling; presumably this gold coin should serve as one pound sterling - both are most likely, but it does not follow from the mere production of such coins. Production in the technical sense creates only coins, but not money. In the first place, then, the guinea was merely a coin that could be considered a commodity, a trade coin, because it traded as commodity. But there must be something else to include this coin in the monetary system: it had to be arranged that the Guinea - at least from the public coffers - should be proclaimed to pay for so many value units, for example for so many shillings. Such an arrangement was missing in 1663; So at that time the Guinea was indeed created as a coin, but not yet inserted into the monetary system of England. Even if the principle was that gold could be indefinitely expressed in guineas, even then bimetallism would not have arisen because this constitution of the money presupposes that the coins of both metals thus created are money - which in 1663 only for the silver coins This was true because the proclamatory validity of Guinea was still lacking.

This trade coin is said to have been paid later on the stock exchange sometimes with 21 1/2 shillings, sometimes even with 30 shillings; her value was unstable, and she did not have validity yet.

The royal coffers are said to have been instructed occasionally to accept the Guinea for as many shillings as they were worth on the market, for example, to 21 1/2 shillings if that was their market price. But this is not a proclamation in our sense; Rather, it is a rule directed to those funds to participate in Guinea trade taking into account the market price. Thus, the appearance of Guinea changed the English coinage, but not the English monetary system, which remained rather untouched.

Without paying attention to the transitions, we look for the time when the Guinea received proclamatory validity and kept it from then on. It happened in 1717; the validity was set at 21 shillings (by a decree of December 22, 1717, see Kalkmann, England's transition to the gold standard, Strasbourg, 1895, pp. 46-49), and it remained so while Guinea existed. The reasons why the validity of 21 schillings was chosen, along with all other circumstances, are completely indifferent, for from now on this validity acts as a law clause. It was ordered that from now on the Guinea should be "given and taken" as 21 shillings - so it was at least taken from the public coffers, and this suffices for its insertion into the English monetary system.

If gold was fundamentally infinitely changeable in guineas, as it seems to have been, then bimetallism had now developed, as Helfferich expertly points out; for the silver remained hylic metal until 1798 (Kalkmann pp. 84-85).

But since bimetallism is only a state of monetary constitution, not a currency in the narrower sense, the question remains open as to which currency prevailed from 1717 onwards. This depends on the behavior of the public purse in their apocentric payments and so can not be taken from books on coinage, not even from the law collection, since it is only an administrative matter. It remains to fill a gap, which extends to about 1774. [Meanwhile, the question has been re-examined by Alfred Schmidt from Essen; he says: "It is not true that the gold currency began in England in 1774, but that happened as early as 1717." Comp. World Economic Archives, Volume 16, Issue 1, page 277. The justification can be found in the following text: Alfred Schmidt, History of English Finance in the 17th and 18th centuries, Strasbourg 1914 (Issue XXXII of the treatises from the Political Science Seminar Strasbourg).]

However, in 1774 (according to Kalkmann, p. 69) a very important innovation takes place: From then on, the silver coins will only be considered as a chart currency in the amount of 25 pounds sterling. So you have become a divisional, but with a very high critical amount. By this it is impossible that the royal coffers, in apocentric traffic, impose silver coins; Therefore, they are no longer current money and for this reason no longer valutary money. Thus, those payments must be made in Guinea - and by this it is clear that in 1774 the gold standard began in England, which from then on continued, while at the same time bimetallism ceased. But he did not stop because the silver was no longer hylic, but because the silver coins were no longer a curant money, but a bargain money.

This gold currency is plateau and - because of the unlimited expression of the gold - also genetically.

Incidentally, in the same year 1774, the guineas, which already showed noticeable wear and tear, were subjected to a new coinage according to the old coinage; This made the gold standard dromic; the fixed price of the gold had been reached, since no treasure trove was levied and the coins were full; Later, when new wear came about, there were at least narrow limits to the price of gold, according to the degree of wear.
So bimetallism did not occur in 1663, but in 1717; and the gold standard came after Alfred Schmidt in 1717, according to our earlier opinion in 1774.

One can imagine that the merchants of the city of London were very inclined to give the value of gold to the valutary position, because for larger payments this kind of money is necessarily more convenient. But it is not the mood of the city that gives rise to the gold standard, but a measure of a regimental nature, perhaps inspired by the merchants, whose public opinion is never enough to carry them out.

Note that in the year 1774 all silver money was transferred to the position of minor coin; In England, therefore, such apparitions are missing as our thaler (since 1871), or like the French silver piece at five francs, which both pieces, as is well known, survived as emergency notes with silver plates after the introduction of the gold standard. In this respect England offers no example.

On the other hand, however, England has another peculiarity: the formerly valued silver money, however, was made a dividend for payments under £ 25; but for payments in excess of £ 25, it was not optional money, but it got into a very strange position, to be described in more detail. Whoever wished to make a supercritical amount in silver coins, was allowed the ounce of silver coins of 5 shillings and 2 pence; so the Troy Pound silver coins - not silver in general - was accepted as payment in the amount of 62 shillings (= 744 pfennigs). This corresponds to the standard according to which the standard silver has been turned into pennies since the 43rd year of the reign of Elizabeth.

That no merchant availed himself of this permission is clear from the outset-for he would have suffered the most tangible damage because of the greatly reduced weight due to wear; In practice, the silver money was only used for payments below 25 pounds sterling. That regulation was only written on paper.

Nevertheless, the process is most remarkable, for theoretically the following situation has been created: for payments of supercritical sums, the silver coins remained a means of payment - which was not money; these coins were decharacterized without ceasing to be a means of payment, for they were retained as morphic-pensatory means of payment, in theory at least !

Here, then, the rare case of the morphic-pensatory means of payment comes to us as a historical phenomenon, for which we have above arbitrarily invented the ducat example (p. The governing Powers had thus become astray in the constitution of the constitution, and resorted to the compensatory payment, but with the obvious intention of refusing to pay this way of payment: one allowed a payment in coins, which for the present case, the amount of supercritical Height was, no money in our sense were! Those silver coins were therefore money for payments below the critical amount and were not money, but still means of payment, for payments above the critical amount - no wonder for us, who have defined the concept of money legally and not technically.

The position of banknotes in England's older financial system would have to be re-examined. The Bank of England is founded in 1694; at first it probably only constituted a private payment community, so that the use of banknotes as a means of payment was restricted to the clientele only. When these notes entered the monetary system of the state, depends on the question of when the public coffers took those notes in payment (ie allow epicenter). That may have happened at the latest when the Bank of England was entrusted with the management of the state's central treasury.

Since this epicenteric assumption, banknotes in the English currency have been the first example of banknotes (as opposed to coins), and have remained so, as purely state cashes have not occurred in England. At the same time they were the earliest example - and probably the only one - of optional money, since the assumption in anepicentric traffic was initially not enforced. Also, they are the first example of provisional (because redeemable) money in England. Furthermore, they were accessory money - in contrast to the value-added money, since the state did not declare it definitive in its apocentric payments: at last it goes without saying that they were a monetary means of payment; and that they - in contrast to the cash money - are to be understood as emergency money. -

Up to the time of the Napoleonic wars cash money was always valued in England; initially cash silver, later cash gold money; in both cases, however, the cash constitution of the valutary money was maintained.

It was not until the time of need that it brought about a change, and that in 1797. The solvency of the Bank of England's notes was abolished because the state had made heavy use of the bank's treasury. The notes remained state money and were even valutary money of the state. Thus, notales money (instead of cash) was valutary position brought. This condition lasted until 1821, after the preparations for the restoration of the gold standard had been made in 1816.

In that period, the gold money was not abolished, because the Guinea remained worth as much as the metal it is made of, also remained definitive money - but was accessory, because the state was no longer willing to make his payments finally in Guinea. The silver money was anyway accessory, since it served as a dividend money.

The paper money that had become valutary - the notes of the bank - no longer had a metallodromic device; admittedly, hylolepsy was still in existence for the metal gold, but the hylophantism for gold had vanished. Therefore, the gold prices fluctuated back and forth and sometimes rose to a fearful height.

An exodromic administration with reference to important neighboring countries never existed in England.

At that time, the rise in the price of gold was pushed to the excessive issuance of banknotes. It must also be borne in mind that the bank was no longer confined to Lombard and discount transactions, as befitted its very essence, but had to come to the assistance of the state with loans [Now compare: Johannes Wolter, Das Staats Geldwesen Englands at the time of the bank restriction (1797 to 1821), 1917 (XXXIII edition of the treatises from the political science seminar to Strasbourg i.E., publishing house of Karl J. Trübner).]. Similar phenomena were later observed in Austria and will be discussed there. It should only be mentioned here how much at that time in England the exchange-rate course had to be disturbed by the fact that the continental blockade of 1807-1813 made the English export almost impossible; and if England then had to pay subsidies to continental states, such as Guinea - which powerful reason was then given for the rise of gold prices!

It is sometimes read that during that state of the paper industry banknotes were never explicitly recognized as a legal tender. A truly supernatural comfort! It arises from the widespread assumption that legal law is the main issue in monetary affairs. One has to ask, however, not what is in the statutory rights, but what the courts do - and there can be no doubt that the courts recognized the payment in banknotes, otherwise they would have to designate all apocentric payments as invalid, and that English Empire would have been divided in itself. -

By a law of 1816, the restoration of the English gold currency was prepared, and this law is still the basis of the English monetary system as far as coins are concerned.

The whole picture is similar for the year 1816: First, a new gold coin was created, the Sovereign; the Guinea was abolished. The reason is very simple; the Guinea had always been worth 21 shillings since 1717; however, it was counted on the pound sterling, which always meant 20 shillings. So there was no coin worth one pound sterling, but one which was 21/20 pound sterling - a great inconvenience to the traffic, which was now to end. Hence the novelty: the sovereign was proposed according to the rule that his value should be equal to 20/21 the value of the guinea; and the sovereign was paid 20 shillings.

The result of this was that the Troy Pound was used to coin standard gold 21/20 * 44 1/2 sovereigns, or what is the same: out of 40 troypounds of standard gold, 1,869 sovereigns were minted; or, what is again the same: the twelfth part of the troy-pound, called the ounce, was applied at 3 pound sterling 17 shillings 10 1/2 pfennigs (3 £ 17 sh 10 1/2 d). As you can see, the new gold money is just different from the old one; the specific metal content has not changed.

The metallists, with their ever-recurrent memories of the Autometallist era, think that such a gold coin as the Sovereign must of course have had 20 shillings, as it had 20/21 of the Guinea's value. For the Chartalist, it is not self-evident; it was based on a special order; for if it had been proclaimed otherwise, the Sovereign would have been different. -

The hylo-drastic arrangements result from the following arrangements, but, as far as the hylo-phantotic branch is concerned, naturally only came into effect after the sovereign (1821) had become valuta: The English Mint must accept any greater amount of gold that is offered to it into

Sovereigns. The gold is first converted into standard gold and then for each ounce - according to the coin foot - 3 £ 17 sh 10 1/2 d - credited and paid out after some time in sovereigns. By the way, according to O. Haupt, the smallest order accepted by the mint is £ 10,000. As a result, the raw gold in the long run can not be lower than it corresponds to the coin foot (so-called coin price).

But it can not stand much higher, because it ensures the importance of the sovereigns by decharacterizing the noticeably undemanding pieces: they lose, after a certain amount of wear and tear, the property of being money and are regarded as mere bars.
Strangely, the damage is borne by the last owner. So as long as the state ensures sovereigns, and indeed for full-weight, the gold can not be above the coin price.

In practice, the Bank of England acts as a mediator in this chrysodromic administration. She pays, and instantly, for the ounce of standard gold 3 £ 17 sh 9 d, when the raw gold is offered to her - that is, a little less than the mint; However, the offering customer avoids any interest loss. Furthermore, it is customary for the bank to have subordinate sovereigns arriving at their treasury cut up and returned to the astonished bearer-de-commoditizing them.
The Sovereign is worth as much as the metal it is made of, and definitely; furthermore, it became valutary at the moment when the Bank of England was compelled to redeem its notes in this kind of money (1821). -

With regard to silver money, the law of 1816 has brought great innovations. Until then, the coin foot consisted of the 43rd year of the reign of Queen Elisabeth, according to which from the pound of standard silver 62 shillings had been coined.

Now, however, 66 shillings were minted from the pound, in crowns (5 sh), half crowns (2 1/2 sh), simple shillings, half and quarter shillings.

This coin base has thus become "lighter" again, but it is the coin's base of the depleted money. For the silver money just described must only be taken in payment of up to 40 shillings; for larger amounts it has no compulsory course; So it's a divisional.

That silver money is not administered argyrodromically. The state is not obliged to buy silver while it is below a certain price; The state does not do it voluntarily, it even takes care of it. It is only as much of this milder coin as it thinks is appropriate for small payments to be done effortlessly. Nor does the state provide for the elimination of the pieces that have become subject. The pieces lose their capacity to be money only by the unrecognizable nature of the character, and new impressions only take place in order to restore the clarity of the character, although the legitimate content is restored, but this is unimportant. -

Since 1833, the notes of the Bank of England have finally been incorporated into the monetary system.

It has been determined that the notes, which by the way may not be smaller than 5 pounds sterling, must under certain circumstances be forced to pay, that is to say have to be accepted on payments that can be made. However, the circumstances are as follows: the payment must not come from the bank. But for all other payments, not made by the bank itself, but by other payers, coercion of acceptance takes place. Who the recipient is is therefore indifferent; on the other hand, the payer must be a different person from the bank.

But even for such payments there is one more condition: the bank must be ready to redeem the notes. In other words, it must pay the owner, at its request and against receipt of the note, the amount stated in sovereigns; as long as it can and does, the banknotes have that compulsory course (limited only in relation to the payer).

That redemption must take place in sovereigns is undoubted, since in England there is only this definite current money; the type of money in which the notes are to be redeemed is thus clearly determined.

This is the English view on the position of banknotes. However, nothing changes in substance when we say that the banknotes have general compulsory course. For one can understand the legal position of the bank as follows: the bank may impose notes, but it must immediately be ready to redeem them at the request of the recipient. Thus, the English banknotes in our sense are current (page 90); but papyroplatic, which is not a contradiction, since the money that is worth as much as the metal it is made of is only recognized by the general assumption of obligation; but they are redeemable (provisional) current money - while the Sovereign is definitely worth as much as the metal it is made of.

How long the sovereign remains valutary depends, as we know, not on laws, but on the fact that the apocentric payments are actually made in it; Of these, England is no exception.

As long as this condition, which is based on the institutions of 1816, is maintained, England has gold currency, firstly in the Plateau, secondly in the genetic and thirdly in the dromic sense.
According to this model, the German Reich established its monetary constitution from 1871 onwards, whereby the older monetary history of England has become, so to speak, the pre-history of the German monetary system.

In principle, England has always been barred for its value-added money, and only once, in the throes of distress, has emergency regulation entered into it. That bar constitution was based first on the hylic metal silver, then on gold, and the transition was probably due to the easy handling of the gold money, perhaps for obstructional reasons.

According to the principle, the monetary constitution was monometallistic; For a short time it was bimetallic, but, as it seems, not out of reflection, but out of uncertainty, giving the gold the hylic position, without immediately taking it away from the silver, so that this constitution has gained no importance. The fact that the gold standard was well-ordered from 1821 onwards served as a model for neighboring countries, but only from 1871 onwards, and in particular gave direction to the exodromic policies of these neighboring countries.

But there is another development going on: while initially there was only value-added money, accessory types of money gradually came into play. In doing so, we pass the time of the Napoleonic Wars, because at that time there was need and not free choice, and therefore only consider the times in which the value of the value-money was barred; These times are partly present, partly after that interlude. Further, we omit the time of the bimetallistic monetary system. After these restrictions, therefore, only the following have to be considered: the accessory money types with Notal constitution. The following examples gradually emerge: the bronze coins of very small values; furthermore, the preserved silver coins, after the abolition of the hyliac characteristic of the silver. (Both the bronze coins and the silver coins were treated as divisive money, but this circumstance is now out of the question.)

Finally, the notes of the Bank of England belong here after they have been accepted by the state, that is, have become state money. These notes, because suitable for larger payments, are the main type of emergency accessory money. Their application is spread so that they play a prominent role in internal traffic.

Not to be forgotten is the incredible increase in the giro payments, which also, albeit in other ways, limits the use of valutary cash inside.

Value-added cash loses its importance for internal traffic to the same degree, but it remains important for foreign traffic, since the properties of the plateau are taken into consideration abroad.

As a result, the valutary cash is becoming more and more. a facility that serves exodromy. This is the case in particular in the present (1905).

The advance of accessory money with a notional constitution in internal traffic, and the growing use of valutary cash for exodromic purposes, is so important that one should not disregard it by emphasizing only the victory of the gold standard over the silver currency.

§ 17. France

The French monetary system is a creation of the First Consul and is based on the Law of the 7th Germinal of the Year XI (March 28, 1803). It is commonly referred to as the system of bimetallism, but this expression is relatively new. The law deals only with the coinage, according to the then view of the monetary system. The notes of the Bank of France, as Papyro Platonic money, are not yet mentioned in it.

The law states that both silver and golden currency coins are struck. In both cases, the coinage is fine 9/10. The coin base is indicated in France after the already alloyed metal, thus after the coin good, not after the fine metal. The monetary unit is known to Franc and was not created at that time, but maintained.

Silver pieces are pronounced in the following denominations: at 5 Fr.; to 2 Fr.; to 1 Fr.; to 3/4 Fr.; to 1/2 Fr.; to 1/4 Fr., in all these cases so that from the kilogram of the silver coinage pieces in the total validity of 200 Fr. be made.

The expression of the silver is unlimited; that is, whoever delivers one kilogram of the silver coinage, receives silver coins in the amount of 200 Fr., but a treasure trove of 3 Fr. is deducted; that is, only 197 Fr. pieces that have become indistinct or have lost their weight below a certain limit are not returned by the public coffers, so that the circulating silver coins are close to being complete.

Of the gold pieces are mainly important: the piece to 20 Fr. and the piece to 10 Fr. From the kilogram of gold coin so many pieces are marked that together they have the validity of 3100 Fr.

Even the expression of the gold is unlimited: who delivers a kilogram of gold coins, receives 3100 Fr. in those pieces under deduction of a treasure trove of 9 Fr., so in fact only 3091 Fr., in gold pieces.

Also gold pieces are, if the character is indistinct or if they have suffered a certain weight loss due to wear, not spent by the public coffers again.

One part by weight of gold, as you can see, is produced 15 1/2 times as many francs in gold coins as are produced from one part by weight of silver in silver coins. This is known to be the origin of the so-called "ratio of 15 1/2 to 1"; It is the ratio of the coinage and is based on the (1803) value of both precious metals, but it is not the value that can change, but the ratio of the currency in francs.

The metal traders, who want to coin one of the precious metals, have to pay attention to the treasure trove when calculating their advantage; For them, therefore, one receives for a part by weight of gold 15.69 times as much francs as for one part by weight of silver. The ratio important to them is thus 15.69 to 1; it is the relationship - not the expression - but the legally regulated purchase of the two metals. -

Of course, there is no compensatory payment in France, despite the strange words that the law begins: "Five grams of silver of the fineness 9/10 represent the monetary unit" (constituent l'unité monétaire). This is only to imply that in the silver coins for each franc of their validity 5 grams of coin-silver are contained. The sentence in its autometallist version is all the more conspicuous since a gold coin containing only gold and copper can never satisfy that demand.

Thus, according to these provisions, there are two kinds of cash (orthotypical) money: the silver and the golden.

The mint coin made of bronze is notal (paratypisch), and remains unnoticed here. The two types of cash money are worth as much as the metal inside, and they are both definite current. Whoever wishes golden things instead of silver money or vice versa must turn to private moneychangers; The state does not, by right, provide an exchange of both types of money against each other, as Landesberger emphasizes so sharply.   That's French bimetallism.

He leaves, as we know, the question quite open, which of the two types of cash is valutary; this depends on how the public coffers behave in apocentric payments, which is decided by administrative orders, which should be examined in more detail. -

The Bank of France, founded in 1800, issues notes; whether they belong to the state money, depends on whether the public funds take those notes in payment (epicentric acceptance constraint), but this happened.

These notes are not cash, but - in our sense - notable money, even if they are redeemable, which was also the case. In ordinary (anepicentric) traffic they have been without acceptance, that is, optional, provisional money in the form of bills.

Since 1848, the Bank of France alone has the privilege of issuing notes. (Here we omit the fact that in February 1848, for the first time since the Bank's existence, the redeemability of the notes was interrupted and the notes received a compulsory course, which ceased on August 5, 1850).

From 1803 to about 1860 the public coffers made their payments in the cash silver; also the redemption of the banknotes took place at that time in this money, which was therefore valutarisch; In that period, therefore, the gold money was accessory (as were the banknotes and not less the bronze divisional money).

But from about 1860 the public coffers, to which we also count the bank of France bank, change this policy; they make their payments in the cash of gold; By doing so, the cash silver money becomes accessory (while banknotes and bronze dividend money, of course, remain accessory).

This envelope, as described earlier, is related to the fact that in the first period the gold, in the last period, the silver was advantageously usable by sale in London. The state acted thus, in the choice of valutary money, for fiscal reasons. -

For silver valued in Italy, there was argyrodromia: silver was accepted at fixed prices; and in the valutary money silver was contained, almost in the prescribed quantity; therefore, the price of silver was almost fixed in such times - for the customers who opposed the state (not for the state).

However, chrysodromia did not exist at such times, as the chrysoleptic institutions persisted, but not the chrysophantics.

In the days of valutary gold, it was the other way around: there was chrysodromia, for gold was freely definable and gold was included in valutary money, almost in the correct amount; So then the gold price was almost fixed.
But argyrodromia did not exist at such times, for although argyrolepsia persisted, argyrophantism was absent.

As has often been mentioned, the state took it for granted that the bimetallistic constitution of the money would soon become the silver currency, sometimes the gold standard, for obstructive reasons. -

One might think that French coinage was equally suited to render service, now for the gold currency, now for the silver currency; but there is a difference: the silver money is more conveniently priced than the gold money, even if a golden piece is added at 5 francs. There is a certain reluctance to produce pieces of gold of lesser content and lesser validity, although by the very addition of copper easily manageable pieces could be made. Therefore, in France, when gold currency prevails, silver coins are used for pieces of lesser value, but this creates a very peculiar danger.

Note that those silver pieces of lesser value under the Law of 1803 are not a divisional money; neither are they necessary, they are bar. But, as long as France has the gold standard, they are, indeed, accessory money; and in this capacity of being accessory money lies the possibility that the silver coins may then receive an internal agio, for reasons of the metal trade: over which the London silver price decides. By 1860, this price was very high, about 61 pence for the ounce of standard silver, and it was advantageous to sell French silver coins as material.

This would not have been a great misfortune if only pieces of high validity had been given, for in their place gold pieces would have entered; but at that time the silver money was at the same time the only one, the denomination of which went down to small amounts, and it threatened, therefore, because of the agios, the danger, indeed it was realized that the small change from the traffic disappeared, whereby great harassment occurred.

The evil was based in the too high specific content of the silver coins.

For this reason, in 1864, the government reduced the specific salary of the pieces to 1/2 fr. and 1/5 fr., and in 1866 also the pieces to 1 fr. and 2 fr. The meal was kept but changed the grain; no more silver of fineness 900/1000, but such of fineness 835/1000 was used for those coins. This is nothing but a reduction of the specific content.

But it was also added that the so changed pieces were legally declared to mint coins: they were only obligatory up to amounts of 50 Fr. for payments of higher amounts, they became optional. This reduction was sufficient to make the agio impossible, and so these coins remained in circulation from then on.

Of course, the silver coins were not freely definable (while the silver piece remained freely debatable at 5 Fr.); From this the further difference arose: the silver pieces for 5 Fr. remained cash money, but in accessory position; however, the smaller silver coins stopped being cash and became distressed, while for other reasons they were also accessory. -

As a result, the necessity of the coin money has been greatly expanded; before, only the bronze coins had been necessary, and now the silver coins of 2 francs and below were added to the emergency deposit. This was a break with the lore of 1803: at that time, the principle was that all coins made of precious metal should be barred; but now, in addition to gold and silver cash, there was also silver emergency money - which, however, was little noticed, since people were calmed by the sight of silver plates. More precisely informed metallists, however, had to regret this development, while the Chartalist feels unmitigated joy, for a manifested evil was now expediently eliminated. -

Thus remained the monetary constitution of France, until the Franco-German war of 1870 brought a tremendous disturbance. Because of the demands that the French state had to make on the bank, the bank's treasury became insufficient.

It was therefore ordered by law on August 12, 1870, that the banknotes were no longer redeemable, and that they should receive general compulsory course. At the same time, in addition to the older grades, 1,000 francs, 500 francs, 100 francs and 50 francs, new smaller pieces were created for 25 Fr., 20 Fr. and even 5 Fr.

These notes (in contrast to coins called - they were so) had become currency (which is judged only after the general assumption obligation) and formed a third kind of currencies, because the silver piece to 5 Frank and all gold pieces still remained currency.

Now it comes to wonder how the state coffers acted in apocentric payments. It is easy to guess that they only paid in banknotes and not in silver, nor in gold. As a result, the banknotes entered valutary position, and both the silver and the golden currency became accessory. It was therefore conceivable that these two types of currency coins would receive premium, namely, when the inter-valutary price of the French paper currency, which had become valutary, fell sufficiently, which depended on pantopolish circumstances. It is very remarkable how small this sinking was: the agio of the gold money should not, according to Lexis, have been much higher than 2 %. This can only be explained by the fact that the sale of French goods abroad was only slightly shaken;

for the fact that the French Government could have taken exodromic measures in the midst of the war is surely out of the question.

The resulting agio, as small as it was, would have been sufficient to drive the two types of currency coins out of the country - if the situation described had lasted long enough; but the war soon came to an end, and France's public credit was borne out of it without any profound injury, so that bonds could be made from whose proceeds the bank could again be endowed with sufficient cash. One seldom thinks of the increased tax burden, without which such a success would have been impossible, as the connection of the Lytrian policy with the services which the state takes over is easily overlooked. -

With the year 1878 the bank was fundamentally redeemed, and only the really insignificant circumstance changed that the forced course of the notes continued, which is the same in England (since 1833) and hardly noticeable because of its redemption. It even has advantages because of the simpler legal situation.

Thus, the banknote was still curage money, but no longer definitive, but provisional. Definitely, as in the past, the silver and the golden curant money were, and according to the principles of 1803, the government could choose in which of these two types of money the accessory note, no longer valutary, should be redeemed. Just as before the war - at least the platitudes of people could not make any difference. -

But in the meantime circumstances had occurred which, although they had not overturned the Lytrian law of 1803, but the associated Lytrian administration; so it had changed for the regimental consideration very significant. To put it bluntly, let us pause for a moment in the paper industry of 1870-77.

At that time, the exchange rate between France and England meant only this: how many francs in banknotes should one give in Paris to receive one pound sterling; but as chrysodromia reigns in England, it could also be said: to obtain the corresponding amount of gold in England. As you know, this course was less favorable for France than it was before August 1870. If one chooses as Pari the coin pari, which exists between French and English gold money - and this choice is very natural, since France had had gold currency at the outbreak of the war - then during the war the French paper money that had become valuta had fallen slightly below par. But since French gold coins are easily convertible into English sovereigns, it could also be said that the paper money had fallen in comparison to French gold coins, which, in our opinion, is to be expressed as follows: the accessory gold money had a positive premium - but only at a low level - obtained, and therefore it was not used in France, despite unchanged validity, in traffic no longer.

But what about the French silver currency, that is, the silver pieces at 5 Fr.? That depended on the London silver prices; as long as they remained at around 60 1/2 pence, these coins, which had also become accessory money, gained a positive premium, and thus also withdrew from payment transactions. As we know, we do not push this for a "value-for-money ratio of silver and gold" which prescribes the economic world, but see the participation of inter-valutary exchange rates between the gold country and the silver countries. Now, the price of silver in England came into play, and shortly before 1876 his status was so low that the French silver money (which had become accessory since 1860) received a negative premium (against banknotes that had become currency). But since, according to the law of 1803, silver was still free in France (of course only in pieces of five francs), silver shipments to France, directed to the mints, now became advantageous, since for the kilogram of coin-silver always 200 Fr., reduced by the sweetheart, could achieve. The argyrolepsia persisted in France, as did chrysolepsy, but the latter is not considered here.

What had ceased in France since 1870 was argyrophantism and Chrysophantism, which was not considered here: the government was not prepared to pay its (apocentric) payments in silver or in gold.

Thus, at that time of paper money, however, the establishment of hylodromia was destroyed; it was neither the still hylic metal silver, nor the still hylic metal gold. Because hylodromia is known to require two different measures, and only one, namely hylolepsy, was left over, while hylophantism had disappeared for both metals.

Chrysolepsy, however, was ineffective, although it persisted, for it was not beneficial to bring gold to the expression, since it lost, so to speak, the agio.

On the other hand, the argyrolepsia offered great advantage to the owner of silver, because it made a profit by placing cheaply bought London silver at the old prices in France at the mints.
The silver traders brought such silver to France and the state had to stamp it out. France was threatened with silver obstruction, whereas from the point of view of the law of 1803 no objection could be raised.

There the French state came to a very different consideration; he did not want to be pushed to the side of the silver countries weakened in trade, in view of the continuing decline in London's silver prices, which would have been infallible if he had tolerated the obstruction in the past and if the silver money had been valutated again. First he decided to avoid the return to the silver currency and secondly to put a stop to the further development of silver money. The latter could not actually happen in the sense of the law of 1803. Nevertheless, in 1876, against the law of 1803, and for the time being without a new law, the administration simply decided to ban the further acceptance of silver at the mints. This is the famous silver closure of 1876, which was also legally pronounced after some time. Thus the bimetallism of 1803 came to an end and this is not recognized only because the French do not genetically judge bimetallism, as we do, but in a platonic way; for they think that his nature consists in the juxtaposition of gold and silver, while this being consists in the juxtaposition of two hylic metals. It is clear that the silver blockage has administratively taken away from silver its ability to be hylical metal, while the gold remained hylic metal (which, however, does not mean that gold currency had now entered because the gold coins remained accessory money until 1878).

The silver currency still in circulation remained in its validity; it was neither physically nor legally abolished (just as little as the gold money). But while the gold money continued to be money-for the gold was hylic metal-even if cash was in an accessory position, it was quite different for the retained silver currency-money: it became a notional (paratypical) curant money; because silver no longer had the property of hylic metal.

Whereas in 1864 and 1866 the silver coins of smaller amount (from 1/5 Fr. to 2 Fr.) had legally become depleted money and genetically for emergency money, now the larger silver coin at 5 Fr. was legally retained as a curant money, but considered genetically turned into emergency money. This represents a new step in the distribution of the emergency allowance, in complete contrast to the emergency disgust of the law of 1803.

The condition was thus after 1876 and before 1878 so: The valutarische money (the indissoluble banknotes) was necessary: all silver money, whether small coin or currency money, was notal, of course, the bronze mint was also emergency. On the other hand, the gold money was still cash, but it was accessory, and because of its positive agios (against the banknotes valutary) it was out of use. The money in circulation in France, therefore, had become quite necessary, in all its species. In particular, in order to repeat this point, the silver piece at 5 Fr. had also become urgent: for being "notal" does not mean that it has become a paper note; it is not meant to be a plateau but a genetic trait. -

In 1878, as mentioned, the banknotes were redeemable; but in what kind of money were they redeemed?

This important point was left to the administration, in accordance with the law of 1803, but everything depends on the interpretation of this law. The administration of the bank put it this way: According to the law of 1803, there are today (1878) still golden and silver currency and one has the choice between the two; so we choose for the redemption of banknotes depending on the convenience of either silver or golden currency. So it has happened since 1878: was always redeemed in currency, which consisted of precious metal.

But the law of 1803 requires even more; Because of the free character of both metals, it is determined that each of these two types of cash should be cash. This point was not taken into account by the administration of the bank. The silver currency had become since 1876 emergency! In fact, a thoroughly exemplary confusion arising from the lack of sufficient conceptualization and appropriate terminology.

Since 1878, therefore, the Bank of France reserves the right to redeem the notes in cash, namely, in gold money, if it is convenient, that is, if its supply of precious metal monetary allowances contains sufficient gold money; but if that treasure of curant money-for it must be said, can not be talked about by metallic money - that is, if that treasure contains only a little gold money, then the bank cashes its notes-with silver emergency money. The bank does not necessarily cash in cash; Of course, this does not notice the layman, for in his half-sleep he rejoices over the redemption in silver pieces for five francs, which were formerly once bar; However, they were barren before 1876, but they have not been there since then.

By the way, I would like to know which merchant, who thinks practically, has any interest in this redemption into silver currency money, in the silver prices that have prevailed since 1878; at the most he may wish such a redemption, in exchange for the notes of 50 francs or 100 francs, coins of a lesser amount (5 francs) into his hand. This type of redemption is monetary policy without any significance. Is it possible to drive out the devil of the emergency payment by the Beelzebub of another subordinate emergency payment? -

The fact that such a redemption is endured and accepted for cash redemption proves, after all, that in the internal traffic the emergency money is quite harmless, otherwise one would have long ago rebelled against it. -

In times of the described redemption in silver currency the bank, however, tends to explain that they want to deliver even golden currency if the recipient wants to make a "premium", for example, of 2 per mille. Those who present notes in the amount of 10,000 francs receive silver money of 10,000 Fr. or, if he really wants to have gold money, he pays 20 Fr .; in other words, he is content with 9980 francs in gold pieces. However, this strange custom protects the treasury of the bank, for no such merchant wants to suffer such a loss unless it is absolutely necessary.

How should one interpret this process? One might say that the gold coin is a currency in all dealings, but the proclamation is changeable, depending on the method of payment: apocentrically used, the piece is a bit more valid than in anapocentric use.

This view seems to be correct, since the bank, when paying in gold, does not use it al marco, that is, it does not use it in a pensatory manner. But then one must recognize in this a chartality with a twofold proclamation, which depends upon the nature of the business.

More importantly, in cases of the gold premium, the one limit of chrysodromia is postponed, for the chrysophantine norm is different; You do not receive as much gold in valutary money as you would without a premium, but less.

This is only found here. It is not a big evil. However, it does have a little effect on the so-called automatic regulation of the inter-valutary exchange rate, namely the exchange rate against the other gold countries which do not operate the premium policy. Shipments of gold coins from France abroad - if required exodromic - are somewhat more difficult. So the premium policy is there primarily for the protection of the cash and not for the regulation of the exchange rate course after the Mint par of exchange, because this is precisely this regulation becomes more difficult.

The French constitution was imitated by smaller neighboring countries; first from Belgium in 1832, then from Switzerland in 1850; but only in terms of coin money. In Switzerland, for example, there was no central bank, despite the French model; In the then completely metallic view of these things, the banknotes were not counted among the state's money because they have paper plates.

However, such a thoroughly understandable imitation does not bring about any synchartism, but homochartism; that is, the institutions of those smaller states are modeled on those of France, but a commonality of the metal money created on both sides does not exist in the legal sense. The Belgian pieces at 1 fr., 5 fr., 20 fr., are not at the same time French money; Nor are the French pieces Belgian money - because on both sides there is still no acceptance of the pieces of the neighboring country. It lacks the regiminal acceptance, be it legally or administratively ordered. Such a homochartism pleases the layman, but remains unimportant to the lawyer.

But as the people judge metallically, the conviction arises, on both sides of the border, that the foreign coins are as good as the native ones; they are therefore accepted without distinction; even the public coffers may do this here and there, and then, as customary, they prepare the synarchism, which appears, as it were, the natural enhancement of homochartism. But if this goal is given, then the states that want to conclude Synchartal contracts must also stipulate by agreement that no deviations from homochartism may be made unilaterally. The contractual determination of homochartism is thus an easily comprehensible prerequisite for the further step leading to synchartaism.

Switzerland gave the impetus for this; At first she reduced the small pieces of silver (to two francs and below) on their own account in their specific content, thus breaking the principle of homochartism; but as the measure was exceedingly expedient, France and Belgium joined in, and on that occasion the Synchartal Treaty, containing the mutual acceptance of the pieces of the Confederate States, was expressly closed, whereas until then it had only actually been acted in the sense of Synchartism.

So the so-called Latin coin bundle, which now arose, originally had the purpose of keeping the silver coins of smaller amount in the Federal territory by reducing the specific content of these pieces; and the mutual acceptance of both the silver pieces as well as the gold pieces was ordered.

When the great decline of the London silver price took place and France in 1876 had first of all discontinued the coinage of the large silver coins, it induced his allies to imitate this measure: first the quality of the silver pieces was quoted at 5 Fr., but then, 1878 completely closed.

In this second period of the covenant, therefore, the hylic property of silver is abolished in the whole union, because of the threatening obstruction which we have already known above.

On the other hand, as is well known, this contract lacks the clause of the consistent choice of valutary money; Very often in Switzerland the gold pieces have been treated as accessories, whereas in France and Belgium they were valutary. That choice is administrative, and the Synchartal treaties did not want to intervene in the administration because each state wanted to remain independent in its administration, as far as the production of the coins was concerned. Therefore, the lytropolitische effect of the contract was not very extensive: the exodromic administration is by no means common to this covenant, but this remained unrecognized, since these metallistically thinking countries had no clear idea of this.

Quite unexpectedly, the Confederation was in a situation that is very strange: it was originally probably synchsal only want to treat the cash types. Already in the first period, however, the small silver coins which had been made useless were subjected to synarchism; and in the second period, when the silver piece had also become necessary at five o'clock, syncheticism was retained for this piece, which remained current money. But this currency was notal. Thus, in addition to the synarchism of cash, to which since the second period only gold has belonged, there has also been synarchism of the silver that has become quite common: while synarchism has never been thought of in regard to the equally necessary papyroplatic money. This circumstance was disregarded because the necessity of the silver money as a mere legal feature was veiled by the unaltered plateau of the silver currency pieces.

That it was advisable, for commercial policy reasons, only to treat the gold money as valuta, was felt to be dark, but not even pronounced for France alone, let alone for the whole Confederation, which did not want to touch this administrative point.

In general, the legal status of synchartal money was misunderstood. It was believed that the Belgian, Swiss, French pieces were still Belgian, Swiss, French money, as they bore the stamp of one or other of these states. There is a superstition about the character, while the character of the mutual acceptance expressed in the contract had become completely indifferent. That money had become federal money, because the legal system is decisive, and not the purely technical circumstance of the character.

Since this was disregarded, one failed to include in the Synchartal Treaty a clause quite necessary, namely, how to keep it, if, for example, the synchartale Federal Covenant, especially the notional currency (ie the silver pieces at 5 Fr.) be replaced by cash currency (ie in gold pieces). But this thought appeared very soon; Because one was averse to the emergency allowance, without being able to say for what reason, the very adventurous plan came out that every state had to exchange the silver currency pieces bearing its stamp for gold money. In this way, Belgium, whose mint was closest to London, and which had been the most heavily used to make silver that had become cheap, would have had a tremendous burden to bear.

Of course, that money had to be recognized as federal money, and the federal government had to devise retrospectively a yardstick for the distribution of the load, for which the scale of the population was the most suitable. Certainly it is only right to do so; while the decision on the character would be quite wrong, because it completely disregards the property of the federal money. Indeed, comparisons have been made, according to which that transformation, if it should be demanded by the Covenant, should be carried out. But the suggestion to decide on the character shows how little one understands in the Latin coin bundle what the content of the treaties really means. As a result, the members have exhausted themselves in barren dispute and enjoyed little joy from their union.

Incidentally, from the point of view of chart theory, it can not be said that homochartism, or even syncharchy, is in itself questionable; these facilities are possible; but they do not readily grant firm, inter-valutary courses, and they may create abundant material for friction, so that they harbor a certain political danger. One realizes, therefore, that in 1871 the German Reich showed little inclination to join the Western Synarchism, especially as the leading state in the West always indicated that it saw in the imitation of its institutions a certain recognition of its ideal supremacy. From a metallistic point of view, this was usually justified by the fact that the neighboring peoples of France adopted the measure of length, the k-per-measure and the metric weight of the French; why are they reluctant to imitate the French coinage system, which has the most rational connection to those measures, that 5 grams of silver of the fineness 9/10 are a Franc, and that 15 1/2 weight units of silver are equal to one weight unit of gold? But it is not true, it must be answered that the Franc is defined by a weight of metal. It is also not true that the value ratio of gold and silver is equal to 15 1/2 to 1. The Frank is an idea of legal life and the means of payment are administratively ordered tools of economic transport, while the meter and liter and kilogram are aids to physical measurements. Therefore, French coinage, as good as it is in itself, can never be recommended for reasons of physics. In lytropolitisch regard, however, it has no preference over the English or German coinage. -

In France, since 1803, the idea has been strictly enforced that the value date should be cash-settled. The exception, which was allowed from 1870-1877, was based on distress and may therefore be ignored here. It is peculiar in the bimetallist constitution that the choice between the two types of cash for valutary use was made entirely at the discretion of the administration, which in turn was guided by obstruction, until in 1876, for exodromic reasons, the hylic took position and thereby finally swung into the way of the gold standard.

In France, too, however, one observes the suppression of valuta cash from internal traffic, first through the inclusion of banknotes in state money, for acceptance by state coffers; This happened very early, but little attention was paid, because in France the means of payment are not expected to be included in the money, since it is paproplastic. In our opinion, however, the banknotes, if they are accepted by public coffers, are part of the public money and are therefore to be mentioned here as accessory emergency money. The bronze coins, though insignificant, are an example of accessory emergency money.
When the silver coins of 2 francs and the even smaller ones, with the specific contents of 5 grams of silver of the fineness, were added, they became accessory emergency money.

This money, which had become necessary, was a divisional money with a very high critical amount (50 Fr.) and could therefore be used heavily in traffic. -

The largest deposit of accessory emergency money, however, took place when, in 1876 in France and in 1878 in the Latin coin bundle, the hylische property was withdrawn from the silver: thus the pieces moved to 5 Fr., which had been accessory but bar, to the accessory emergency money on. Not as if new money had been created! This currency was also there before, and it remained; but it lost the quality of being barred and became necessary, which the layman did not notice.

It is said that in France in 1896 there was a stock of these pieces in the amount of 2,000 million francs. (A history of banking in all the leading nations, Vol. III, 1896, page 90.)
This has proved to France, too, that the value of current currency in the interior is always losing in favor of the emergency money, and that it is increasingly putting itself in the service of exodromic purposes.

§ 18a. German Empire in 1905

The German Reich as a federal state has legislation that is well distinguishable from the legislation of the individual states. The legislation of the individual states basically has nothing to do with the monetary system; On the contrary, finance belongs to the Reich, which is known to be responsible for coinage, cash for banknotes and banking.

The German Reich has no mint; these technical institutions belong, as before, to the countries; however, they work according to the instructions of the Reich. The mints are: A. in Berlin; (B. in Hanover, C. in Frankfurt a.m.) D. in Munich; E. in the Muldenerhütte near Freiberg in Saxony, formerly in Dresden; In Stuttgart; G in Karlsruhe; (H. in Darmstadt); J. in Hamburg. The brackets mean that the activity is discontinued. The enclosed letters are printed on the coins to indicate the place of manufacture.

It is known that the image of the sovereigns and the emblem of the three free cities on the imperial coins of 2 marks and more is valid - which has no meaning and only happens in order not to abolish an old custom out of courtesy.

The following can be considered for the administration of money: the mints, insofar as they have to accept commissions for imprints; and the Reichsbank, which has taken on many duties on behalf of the Reich; and finally the public coffers in the German Reich - whether they be funds of the Reich or the Länder - because of the regulations on which types of money to accept and spend.

- The legislation of the empire begins with the law on the expression of imperial gold coins of December 4, 1871: it is clearly collected in the work of Koch and in other works to which reference must be made here; because for us it is only a question of theoretically summarizing the result.

Since 1876, through reforms that began in 1871, our lytric constitution has been so developed: our unit of value, called the Mark, is defined as the third part of the previously customary value unit of Thalers. We do not know any pessatory payment; chart payments are predominant; Giral payments are often made through the intermediary of banks.

For the Reich money we count, since the Reich is a Zahlgemeinschaft, all those currency-based means of payment, which with the central office, that is with the Reichsbank, recognize acceptance, thus are "accepted"; From this it follows that we have seven types of money, which are to be listed first, stating their denomination:

1. The gold coin, called the crown, completed to 10 M. And the other gold coin, called double crown, completed to 20 M .; the names crown and double crown are little in use, because they are not attached to the pieces.

2. The Silver Coins stamped according to Imperial Law: pieces with the validity 5 M., 2 M., 1 M. and 1/2 M.

3. The nickel coins, to 10 Pf. And to 5 Pf. Pfennig means the 100th part of the Mark; furthermore the copper coins to 2 Pf, and to 1 Pf.

4. The Taler, a silver coin with the validity of 3 M., originating from the former monetary constitution.

5. The Reich Treasury notes; there are pieces of 50 M, 20 M and 5 M.

6. The notes of the Reichsbank; there are pieces of 1000 M and 100 M.

7. The notes of some privileged banks; here are the pieces to 100 M. the only ones.

The money types 1.-4. are coins; the money types 5 to 7 are bills.

Since 1871 we have the following basis of the monetary system: there is only one hylic metal, the gold; So there is only one kind of cash, the above-mentioned gold coins.
These gold coins have been valuta money since 1876, but this is based only on the fact that since that year the Reichsbank makes its apocentric payments at the request of the recipient in gold; since then we have gold currency in the platonic and genetic sense. As much as this is in accordance with the intention of our legislation, it is based only on a legal basis, more precisely on an administrative order, since the Reichsbank is not compelled by law to do so. -

The constitution of the above seven types of money is arranged as follows:

1. The gold coins are made of gold of the fineness 9/10. Basically, any amount of gold is unlimited in double crowns cantilever; and indeed, from the pound of fine gold 1395 marks are made in double crowns; this is the hylogenic norm. The double crowns and the crowns are cash money, since their specific content 1/1395 pounds is fine, thus in

accordance with the hylogenic norm. Also, they are currency, since you have to accept any payment that can be made in this money. Furthermore, they are definite money, because they do not have to be redeemed in any other kind of money. The fact that they have been valutary money since 1876 is based on the fact already mentioned that the Reichsbank and the other public coffers are, in the final analysis, prepared to make their payments in this gold money; Of course, we are talking only about payments of critical and supercritical amount.

For payments to public coffers, ie for epicenter payments, the actual value is irrelevant. In the case of apocentric payments, on the other hand, no pieces are used which are more worn down than up to 995/1000 of the prescribed weight. In anepicentric traffic, the pieces sunk below the passing weight are no longer valid. Nevertheless, the gold coins are proclamatory.

2. Since the silver has not been a hylic metal since 1871, the silver coins are not cash (orthotypical), but not (paratypical) money. It is made of silver of fineness 9/10 and its specific content is 1/100 pounds of fine silver, that is to say that for every cent of its value it contains 1/100 pounds of fine silver; That this is no justification for their validity, but only an accompanying circumstance, is often mentioned. Their manufacture is reserved and restricted to the Reich: only 10 M may be produced, according to a later rule 15 M on the head of the population. Since larger apocentric payments in these coins are not intrusive, they are not value added but accessory money. For epicenter payments, their use is unlimited. In apocentric and paracentric traffic they must be accepted up to the amount of 20 M; the critical height is thus 20 M .: they are divisional money. In amounts of 200 marks and more, they are redeemable in gold money; for the redemption 200 M. is the critical height.

The solvency is not the reason for their validity; Like all money, they are proclaimed, and would continue to operate undisturbed if their solvency no longer existed. Metallistic theory, which does not know the proclamation of validity, wrongly considers the solvency of the reason for the validity of this means of payment.

3. The nickel and copper coins are legally only one type of money, despite their technical differences.

The nickel coins are made from a mixture of 75 parts copper and 25 parts nickel (a type of brass whose low nickel content hardly justifies the name of these coins and robs them of the beautiful appearance of real nickel coins). Of the 5 pfennig pieces, 200 will go on the pound, of the 10 pfennig pieces (not 100, but) 125 pieces.

The copper coins are made from a mixture of 95 parts copper, 4 parts tin, 1 part zinc. It is characterized from one pound: 1-Pfennig piece 250; but 2-penny pieces (not 125, but) 150.

Of course, they are not cash but not necessarily money.

Their production is also contingent (2 1/2 M. on the head of the population). They are not valutarian, but accessory money, for the same reason as the Reich silver money. For epicenter payments, they should not be used indefinitely, which is actually illogical. For all payments, they must be accepted up to the critical amount of 1 M; they are so divisional money.

In amounts of 50 marks and more they are redeemable in gold money; in this respect 50 M. is the critical height; Here, too, the solubility has nothing to do with validity, just as little as the metal content.

4. The taler is taken from the previous constitution, ie not in accordance with the rules of the current constitution; it is Reich money, but not according to the Reich relevant law. There are two varieties: before 1857, 14 Talers were made from the "mark" of fine silver; the Cologne mark, a weight unit, is given as 233.8555 grams.

This variety is little in circulation, although it still has validity. The other variety is pronounced according to the law of 1857: the taler contains 1/30 pound of fine silver; the coinage is 9/10 fine. The specific content, based on the value unit mark, is therefore 1/90 pounds of fine silver (while the specific content of the Reich silver coins is 1/100 pounds of fine silver). The specific value of the Thaler is therefore greater than that of the imperial silver coins - which is irrelevant, since the validity is not based on the value.

Since the Taler used to be valuta money, and since it is still preserved, it may be called exvalutarian.

The taler is not cash, because silver is no longer hylic metal; it is notale money (despite the fact that silver is counted among the precious metals) just like the Reich silver coins.

It is not value-money either, since the public coffers, especially the Reichsbank, do not impose it on their apocentric payments, although they may do so under the law; So he belongs to the accessory money. Only in memory of the former valutarian position we call the Taler exvalutary.

The taler is, however, still, currency, because legally he is with all payments that can be made in it, necessarily accept, just as our gold money. It is due to this circumstance that our monetary system is often referred to as a limping currency; but this can only happen to those who judge a monetary constitution according to the type of cash, not to the hylic status of the metals.

By law, the taler is definite money, since it is not redeemable; but administratively it is redeemable; We have to reckon on the redeemable, that is provisional, types of money, as we judge by the law of the law.

By all accounts the taler will gradually disappear; Since one can produce just 100 marks in Reich silver coin from 90 Marks in Taler, the empire financially has a great advantage by transformation of the Taler piece in Reich silver coin, whose contingent has therefore been increased. If this transformation had already taken place, our monetary system would be somewhat simpler; but the emergency money would not be limited and the subvalence (the negative premium) would be even greater than before.

Only the clarity of our monetary system would gain what you put a lot of weight. But a really serious question is not this. For only the Metallists have the Notre-Shy and are dominated by the tobacco addiction, which had the highest spread from the beginning of the 19th century to about 1857.

The taler money is locked since 1871.

The coins with Austrian character, to be discussed later, were valid until the end of 1900 in the German Reich; Part of this was taken over by the Austrian Government as a result of a retrospective settlement, since the Synfac contract of 1857 of course did not state how the burden was to be distributed in the transition to a completely different currency.

5. The Reich Treasury notes (Reichskassenscheine), created by the law of April 30, 1874, are part of the money, because they are to be taken from all public coffers in payment, including the central office; since they are bills (not coins), they can only belong to the emergency money; but they are also not hylogenic money, because there is no need to deposit hylic metal (that is, gold); so they are autogenic.

In anepicentric traffic they have no assumption obligation, so they belong to purely optional money; they are not to be added to the currency or the divisional. They are redeemable in cash at the Reich Central Fund; but whether the law has the same concept of money as we do is very doubtful; I suspect that this means coinsmithed money, namely a mint coin, if the amount has only the critical amount of 20 marks or less, and currency coins (ie coins or gold coins), if the amount is greater; whereby then on the Taler excrete

because the bank imposed on administrative order no Taler (since about 1876). However, this is factually the same: namely redemption in cash according to our terminology as soon as the amount exceeds the critical level. Accordingly, the cash-notes are provisional (not definite) money.

Redeemability is not ensured by a prepared fund; even if it were, it would not be the reason for the validity, for here too the validity is proclamatory.

The law allows only a total amount of 120 million marks to be made in these notes, so this type of money is blocked, but this does not affect its validity.

It is known that the Reich kept a treasure of 120 million Marks, stored up for war, in the Julius tower at Spandau; but this has nothing to do with the Reichskassenscheine; in the legal sense that treasure does not cover these notes.

The very general custom of accepting this optional money even in anepicentric commerce is based on the fact that bills are popular because of their convenient handling; that is why they have never been heard of jamming in the public coffers, although they could very well cause congestion as accessory (not valutary) money and as money with negative agio, as soon as they were unpopular.

The solubility contributes to their popularity, which has not experienced any interruption with us.

6. The Reichsbank (Law of March 14, 1875) corresponds to the above description of these institutions. She issues notes, that is, she creates these notes as a means of payment for her own purposes. These notes are already part of the money, because they are usable by virtue of their definition for payments to the bank, that is to the central office. This money is not hylogenic, but autogenous, for the bank does not have to deposit the entire amount of the notes issued in cash, as we have defined this term. The notes are in our sense notale money (not cash), which

already follows from their property as notes; while the concept of emergency money is by no means limited to notes.

The fact that these notes are also accepted by other public coffers, not only by the central office, is not based on law, but on the administrative arrangement of the Reich and state administrations; after all, it is based on a regimental arrangement and this is enough to ensure their widespread use in traffic. The notes are (in anepicentric traffic) purely facultative money, thus neither currency, nor divisional; they are also redeemable, and the law requires redemption; so they are provisional, not definitive money. But if the solvency ceased, the assumption would still remain at the central office; even with the other public coffers, the assumption would have to be prohibited only in a regimental way. The redeemability is therefore arranged, but it is not the reason for acceptance in public coffers, but only the assumption that the assumption continues there. But if the redeemability ceases, the Reich Government would certainly be guilty of it, and then, as has happened everywhere, further acceptance by public coffers would be prescribed by a special order of a regimental nature.

But so far we have not had that experience.

Because of the redeemability, that is, because the notes are only makeshift money, their valutary use is not present; the notes belong to the accessory money. That they have negative agio is clear from the definition of this concept; therefore they could easily pile up in the public coffers, but one hears nothing about them, because in traffic they are popular, for the same reasons that we mentioned in the cash registers. Therefore, they are safely accepted even in anepicentric traffic. They will only be submitted for redemption if the holder has special reasons for exchanging other types of money, for example due to denominations or because they are being sent abroad.

The issue of notes is unlimited for the Reichsbank and only made difficult by a certain amount because then a tax must be paid to the Reich. It should be noted, however, that the Reichsbank is limited to very specific business; it is not, therefore, an institution that can create and use these means of payment indefinitely and to any business: it is limited in its business, but not limited in the creation of means of payment for the narrow circle of businesses. The nature of these transactions means that this bank can not be in danger of losing its ability to pay unless the state interferes with its operation, as it does in times of need; but then the bank would change its nature.

As everywhere else, the use of emergency money (instead of cash) in internal traffic has received a tremendous boost from the reception of Reichsbank notes under state money.

We still have to ask in which types of money the notes are redeemable; apparently in definitive ways, that is, according to the position of our legislation, either in taler or in gold pieces.

But since the taler is not imposed on us according to our administrative order, those notes are redeemable in gold money; So, in our sense, we have redeemability in cash (to which the thalers do not belong). -

A special concern of our legislation is directed to the so-called covering of notes, that is, other types of money in the cash register of the Reichsbank should be kept in stock, apparently to secure the redemption of notes more. At least one-third of the amount of the notes in circulation should be available at all times in the fund, namely: "in eligible German money with the inclusion of cash in hand" or in gold; the gold can consist of bars or foreign coins and is credited with 1392 marks for the pound.

It is not left to the bank, as it wants to ensure the solvency, but she stand before this special kind of "cover".

But a cover by cash money is this only so far, as that supply exists in German gold money; It is therefore not obligatory that the cover, more precisely the third-party cover, be made entirely by cash; because all other "price-capable money types" are necessary and they are all, at least administratively considered, redeemable themselves. The likewise permissible gold (bars or foreign coins), however, is easily convertible into German gold coins, because of the free expression, so the equal coverage can be equal.

But as far as the emergency money types are concerned (nickel and copper coins, imperial silver coins, thalers, banknotes), no one can understand how they should contribute to the bar-covering of the notes. This part of the rule is explained only by the theoretical uncertainty of the legislator, and as far as it concerns emergency coins, the reverence for metal plates. The shortcomings of these provisions would be very serious if the precise provision on the nature of the cover were required - which it is not, however, as the bank is required by its own interests to be prepared to redeem.

Even the expression "price-able German money" is strange; is there money that can not be traded, which means that there would be no epicenter acceptance obligation? For us, the course ability is not even to mention; Perhaps the legislator wanted to suggest that he did not want to speak here of the general, but only of the epicentric assumption of compulsion.

7. There are in the German Reich a number of banks which in the past already had the privilege of issuing notes; The following are still to be found: the Bavarian Central Bank, the Saxon Bank in Dresden, the Württembergische Bank, the Badische Bank and the Brunswick Bank. One did not want to abolish these privileges, so that we now still have notes of these institutions in circulation. But according to our definition, the notes belong to the money types of the German Reich only if they can make payments to the central office, that is to the Reichsbank.

This position was granted to those banks that submitted to the banking law, ie, above all, restricted their business in the familiar way.

This has not been done by the Braunschweigische Bank. Their grades are therefore only money for their clientele or, if the Brunswick public coffers accept these notes, then those notes are the only example of -

state money, in contrast to Reichsgeld. The Reichspost accepts those notes for instructions within the Duchy; It regards them as state money. (Incidentally, the said bank renounced its note issue on December 14, 1905.)

The other Landesbanks, on the other hand, are subject to the Banking Act; their notes are therefore taken into payment at the Reichsbank and are thus in our sense, because of this acceptance, a kind of Reichsgeld. However, the Reichsbank shifts these foreign notes to the issuing office to redeem or credit the amount. From this, however, follows for us only that there is Reichsgeld, which indeed enjoys the acceptance, but is issued neither by the Reichsbank, nor by all public coffers (but perhaps by those of the countries concerned): purely acceptance Reichsgeld.

For the rest, the law of these notes is quite similar to that of the Reichsbank notes; they are necessary money; redeemable (ie provisional) money; optional money; of course also accessory money. Deviating is only this: they are blocking money, since the note issue of all these banks (as well as the Brunswick bank) is limited to an absolute amount. -

To describe our monetary condition, we must also have hylodromia, chrysodromia; this follows from the unrestricted acceptance of gold for conversion into money and, secondly, from the valutary position of the gold money, whereby the owner of other types of money can always obtain gold.

Finally, we have exodromics, when disruptions of the exchange rate policy against the gold countries make it necessary, through so-called discount and Lombard policies.

From the English model we deviate only in subordinate points: decimal division of the mark; nominal metal plated currency (Taler); Admission of cashier's notes; Position of the banks, which exist alongside the central bank; but otherwise the imitation is almost complete.

So we have gold currency in the platonic, in the genetic and in the dromic sense; but more than that, we have a tremendously widespread use of the emergency money in internal traffic, where the cash money would withdraw even more if it were not so much supported by the denomination; and finally: we have an exodromic administration where cash is its main use.

§ 18 b. German Empire; Transition from 1871 to 1876

The transition to the present constitution of the monetary system can in short in such a way be represented :
Before 1871, more precisely before the foundation of the German Reich, there was of course no Reichsgeld, but only money of the individual countries. The monetary system of the countries, however, was governed by treaties, so that it was far from actual extermination. The last state treaty, which we have alone to consider, was that of 1857: the so-called German-Austrian Coin Club. It was closed between the states of the Zollverein on the one hand and the Austrian imperial state on the other. As far as Austria was concerned, this state treaty is to be discussed later.

For the states of the Zollverein (customs union of German states established in 1833) the following was the essential content.

At first it was considered that only the money minted was real money. **There were, in the individual countries, cash-notes, to which at least the epicentric assumption obligation was added**; there were also banknotes, some of which were also taken over by administrative orders from public funds.

But the treaties were content to say that these kinds of money should not be given general coercion in case of irredeemability. For the rest, however, the bills were excluded from the agreements. Only the coin money was the subject of the appointment. -

The condition he had developed after 1857 is easy to overlook, if we only highlight the main points.

For this purpose we let withdraw the complicated mechanisms of the coinage, which are only of minor importance, and consider only the currency. Then the following simple picture emerges for the older state of the states of the Zollverein.

There were two groups of countries: in northern Germany, the group with taler money; and in southern Germany the group with gulden money. The gulden countries were: Bavaria, Württemberg, Baden, Grand Duchy of Hesse, Hohenzollern (since 1849 under Prussian rule), Saxe-Meiningen, Saxe-Coburg, Schwarzburg-Rudolstadt-Oberherrschaft.

In the Taler countries the Taler was currency; We have often mentioned the coin base of this piece.
In the gulden countries the gulden was currency. According to an earlier regulation, 24 1/2 guilders were made from the Cologne mark of fine silver; From 1857 on 52 1/2 guilders were stamped from the pound of fine silver. Again, there is a small difference, but was also practically neglected.
So 4 talers, according to their content, were equal to 7 guilders.
Now, however, the important provision was added in 1857: the gulden countries were also to design coins of the newer type in addition to the gulden of the newer type. From then on there were also Bavarian, Württemberg, Baden thalers, and so on.
And all thalers should be allowed in the association area with all payments; Therefore, the new taler wore the name Vereinstaler.
The quality of being a current money was attached to all the pieces whose specific content corresponded to that of the thalers: the simple thalers, the double thalers, the Saxon thirds, and even the sixteenths; furthermore, with restriction to the southern group of states, the simple gulden piece, the double and the half gulden piece.
This currency was cash money, because it was everywhere the principle that silver was unlimited in currency worth as much as the metal it is

made of. Hylic metal is therefore the silver, and only the silver. The expression of gold to so-called Zollverein-Crown was permitted, but this coin was a trade coin, so no money.

All the states of the Zollverein (to which Austria is known not to belong) had the principle of making their apocentric payments in that silver currency; therefore that silver money was valutary. There was also accredited coins, but only as a dividend, which we will mention for the sake of brevity here. The bills (partly cashier's notes, partly banknotes) were not ordained by law, but stood alone under the national legislation. In the states of the Zollverein, therefore, one had silver currency, first in the sense of the Plateau, secondly in the genetic sense; and since the states in apocentric traffic no longer spent the currency, when the actual value had fallen below the passing weight, the silver currency was also in the dromic sense. -

Without unduly praising the described older state, one may argue that he was not absolutely unbearable. So much has been achieved in coinage as one might expect from independent states, that is, when the bureaucracy of the countries, without transition to a federal constitution of the whole, could prevail. At first there was no reason to leave the silver currency. Greater simplicity would have been welcome, of course, but the main points had been reached. Because of lasting peacetime, the bills could not be questionable, since all states had an instinctive aversion to the paper money economy, whose unseen daily saw in the Austrian imperial state in mind; and the proliferation of private banks with notes issued only after 1857.

The evil did not consist in the mismanagement of the independent states, but in the immobility of the Union of States, which lacked the constitution by which one could have come to even simpler states. But the simplicity was lacking, as the South German guilder still existed and in northern Germany the coins were not alike everywhere.

These defects, from a higher point of view actually quite subordinate, but have the property of being very noticeable in ordinary life. On a railway journey from north to south, or vice versa, every traveler had the annoying experience that the mint and gulden were not uniform. The wholesale trade did not notice that; but the small traffic suffered a lot, and the small traffic dominates the mood. One was therefore dissatisfied with the condition, because the petty evils, which were in themselves troublesome, came to the fore.

Moreover, everyone in the paper knew that every step further elicited the most pervasive friction between states, while all the educated were fully convinced that all the states (Switzerland, North America) were organizing their finances by federal legislation. Thus, with the creation of the German Reich, it could not be denied that money would be raised to the cause of the Reich - and it is well known that this happened immediately. -

It is now necessary to examine in which seasons the constitutional order of our monetary system has taken place.

Of course, the generally prevailing view holds itself to the visible, and above all speaks of the expression of the gold coins which today form our kronengeld; It is supported by the undeniable fact that our first Reichsgesetz already emphasizes in the title the form of gold coins.

Not only the public, but also the legislature is metallic through and through, how should the writers not be! But think of all the mints as busy as possible with the production of gold coins - this does not change the monetary constitution, which indeed belongs to the field of legal life.

Rather, the first step is that the monetary system was declared a matter of the Reich and thus withdrawn from the lands.

This is followed by the soon to be added provision: the old coin money will be exchanged in the future by the Reich (not by the

countries) against the new coin money. It is expressed in these facts that from now on all the existing stock of old money should be regarded as Reichsgeld. The Reich, so to speak, adopts the old money, then later abolish it and put it in its place. So at that moment there was already Reichsgeld; not only the expression of the new gold creates Reichsgeld; it creates much more new Reichsgeld, and that Reich coins, that is coins, according to the laws of the empire coined / shaped. But the first Reichsgeld are the old coins of the country, which explains the Reich as its money, to abolish later.

That these old coins did not carry the stamp of the empire is quite indifferent; the stamp is only a mark, which expediently indicates at the same time who exercises control over money; but that is not necessary, for there is nothing to prevent it from adding a new meaning to the old mark, for which purpose a rallying of the ruling powers suffices. The rally is that the administration of the monetary system is transferred to the Reich; The old money becomes thereby money of the realm, because under it not the private-law possession of the money, but the public-juridical control of the monetary system is understood. Quite similar was already the case with the Krontalers (Crown-Thalers) in southern Germany: they were money in the gulden countries (proclaimed to 2 7/10 gulden) although they came from the mints of the Austrian Netherlands and bore the appropriate stamp.

Thus, the old money had first become Reichsgeld through that adoption, and the Reich soon set up a new kind of money next to it, the golden kronengeld. To make it useful for traffic, it was said: we call the third-taler now Mark; and our gold pieces are 10 marks or 20 marks, and so they are to be accepted in all payments; but also the old money remains for the time being in the previous usability, until explicit disclaimer occurs.

For the Chartalist, nothing is particularly peculiar.

Thus, from 1871 onwards, there were two kinds of "currency": the old one with silver plates and the new one with golden plates. If one wishes to call this bimetallism, it must be added that it was only a platistic bimetallism; however, it was not genetic because the silver was immediately taken the hylical property while it was given to the gold. But from this follows: From now on only the new gold money was cash; the old silver currency money, which had remained in circulation for some time, had become urgent. As strange as that sounds to the metallist, it is nonetheless true: from 1871 the taler and the gulden were notales (paratypical) money with silver plates.

As a result, the Argyrodromie also came to an end, and with her the importance of passing weight for the silver currency stopped.

On the other hand, chrysodromia did not occur immediately, as might be expected. For at that time inexperience had been neglected to make a provision on the valutary use of the two types of currency. The public coffers, on the whole, remained in the tradition, that is, they usually paid in silver currency, and only occasionally, if they chose, were they prepared to pay in new gold. This means, however, that after 1871, and until 1876, we had a provisional constitution of valutary money; the Notal pieces, however, were argyroplatic, but they were still emergency. It is very strange that this state is not called by the right name. Pay attention only to the condition of the plates! It is further thought that at that time one had still silver currency, because the gold currency had not yet been carried out - just as if there could be only cash constitution for the valutary money, as long as no paper economy exists. This is quite wrong; it can also give valutary money consisting of notable silver coins, and we had that condition at that time. -

The origin of the base of the coin for the crown money ("crowns" and "double crowns") explains itself as follows: When one decided to create the crown money, was in the relevant market for silver, namely in London, the price of silver so that one for 1 weight unit of fine gold, contained in sovereigns, could purchase just 15 1/2 of weight units of fine silver in ingots. According to the same ratio, the metals gold and silver in francs have been pronounced in France since 1803. This ratio was therefore considered from 1803 to 1871 as the so-called normal.

Some people believed it had to be and stay that way. It was considered as one sentence of experience that gold was 15 1/2 times as valuable as silver, with equal weights, especially since it was so found in 1871!

If new gold coins were to be created, it was taken for granted that their coin base should be set up so that the specific plate value of the new pieces would be equal to that of the old one.

Thus, if the taler was proclaimed three marks, and the crown was to be proclaimed 10 marks, the coin's base of the crown was found to be 1395 = 3 times 30 times 15 1/2 marks in crowns because from the pound of fine silver 90 = 3 times 30 marks had been marked in talers. This is known to be the origin of our coin foot for the Kronengeld. The reasoning was then readily accepted as valid, since it corresponded to the autometallist conception, as if one were actually transmitting metal coins; At the same time, however, it is based on the idea that the two metals possess that value relation as a permanent property, which is not the case at all. After all, it was possible to enforce the mentioned coin foot without resistance.

The weak side of the autometallistischen reasoning of the coin foot for the Kronengeld is quite unmistakable: neither you paid until 1871 with silver in itself, you still paid later with gold in itself.

Chartalistically, the step should have been justified in this way: So far our money, consisting of pieces of silver, was administered argyrodromically; Now, on the other hand, we want to move on to a chrysodromic monetary entity through the mediation of the crown money to which we procure chrysodromism. In order for the transition from argyrodromia to chrysodromia to take place without jerking, that is, following the value relationship that existed at the time (1871), the coin foot must be chosen for the new crown money to be created, which has indeed been chosen: 1395 marks in Crown money from the pounds of fine gold.

Here the basis of coinage is not justified by the fact that 15 1/2 pounds of silver are in themselves worth as much as a pound of gold; but by the fact that the choice of another coin foot would have produced a jerk in the exchange rates between England and the German Reich; but this really chosen coin base guaranteed the continuation of the then existing exchange rate, more exactly the rate-based exchange rate. -

The progress of the reform was now thought of in such a way that gradually the old silver money should be confiscated and replaced by the new kroner money: thus one would have arrived at a uniform, initially platonic, gold standard.

Certain types of old money have continued to be accepted by the public purse but have not been reissued: that is silent confiscation. Then it was declared that certain old types of money were redeemable in new money up to and including the time: that is call-in; after the deadline, they should lose the general compulsory course, but still keep the epicenter. At last it was said that from a certain moment on the old pieces would be completely deprived of the property of being money; that is disclaimer. Due to the disclaimer, the old silver coins turn into ingots, which, however, by chance, still bear a stamp; the character then has no meaning.

The time of the disclaimer occurred:
1874 for the Krontaler (silver pieces, proclaimed to 2 7/10 guilders, originating from the Austrian Netherlands, then very common in southern Germany);
In 1874 for the half and whole gulden pieces;
1876 for the two-thaler pieces and the third-thaler pieces;
1878 for the sixth-thaler pieces;
1900 for the Austrian Vereinstaler (minted after the Treaty of 1857); they retire at the end of the said year, so they are no longer Reich money. (In Austria they had been suspended since June 1, 1893).

In this way, to mention only the most important types of money, and without regard to the small coins that we pass over here, the situation was considerably simplified.

But of the old types of money, one, the most important one, is not collected, not called in, and not called: the pieces of the taler, or more precisely the pieces of a thaler, have remained in circulation, as far as they come from countries of the Zollverein. Their legal status remained unchanged; they remained the common currency of the Reich, what they had already become in 1871; and next to the crown money. It is well known that because of the decline in silver prices which had occurred in the meantime, it was intended to avoid the loss of the finances of the empire that would have arisen when the Talersilver was sold.

Since this type of money continued to exist next to the crown money and still exists (1905), we still have a limping currency, as is customary in the case of a French writer.

Is this a fault or not?

Anyone who considers reform as a goal, that there should be only one mundane, namely the golden one, must regard the limping currency as an imperfection, as most people do.

But whoever regards as the goal of the reform that we carry out the gold standard in the Platonic, genetic, and dromic sense, the continuation of the silver Kurantgeldes, ie the Talers, is completely indifferent, provided that the Talergelde is given an accessory position. But this was not done first (1871).

So not in the continued existence of the Talers as Kurantgeld lies the imperfection of the reform; but in the missed measure to make the taler accessory; but this does not necessarily mean that he should have been given the draft of the mint, although that would have sufficed; It would only have been necessary to eliminate the enforceability of the taler in apocentric traffic - and so it was done by administrative means in 1876.

But let us dwell for a moment on the period 1871-1876.

As long as the taler money was valutary treated, the new gold money was, despite all good intentions for the future, accessory; as such, however, an agio could very well be obtained, for this phenomenon occurs with accessory money, and indeed when its use in the plant is more advantageous than the lytric one. Money with a positive premium but disappears from the traffic. Our Reich government thus always had new gold coins stamped under circumstances which made it conceivable that new money would immediately be treated as a commodity and put out of circulation - because the new golden money has an accessory position.

In fact, this occurred in 1874. At that time the pound of gold, paid in talers, cost not 1395 marks, but more, up to 1410 marks. There is nothing puzzling about that. It would be incomprehensible only if the pound of gold had cost 1410 marks in crowns, at that time the absolute value of the crown money. But this was not the case: it cost 1410 marks in thalers.

At that time had the Kronengeld - a small agio and was executed! The people were surprised because it was currency. But that does not matter. It had just not been valutary money. This term, unknown as the underlying term, was still missing and replaced by a barrage of words.

Even the quantity theory has been and still is set in motion to explain that phenomenon. The new gold money, in addition to the taler money, is said to have created an overabundance of money, so that it had to sink in price against English money! But not the increase of the money supply per se is effective; but the irresponsible use of money in payment transactions, more precisely, the failure to consider valutary the gold money.

One sees it by the measure, which brought the healing. Already in 1875, says E. Nasse, the Prussian bank was "so intelligent" to pay on request in crown pieces (writings of the Association for Social Policy Bd. XI, 1875, page 212). And in 1876, the Reichsbank went to the practice of treating the gold money as valutary and change all accessory money at the request of the owner in valutary money, including taler for krona money.

Immediately the high price of the gold disappeared and with it the premium of the crown money. The Reichsbank was "intelligent" at that time because it instinctively did what no theory at that time knew how to say in simple terms. We have stayed with this exercise and, as we have already said, without the legislation requiring it, which is undoubtedly a gap, but voluntary exercise is sufficient for transport. -

The whole monetary reform has been started and carried out with us in unclear keys. The real merit belongs to the practitioners, who always found ways to enforce the Chrysoplatic and Chrysodromic currency, while the legislature was not actually thinking of monetary reform, but only of coin reform. It was believed that the meager distinction between the Kurantgeld and the Scheidegeld, and the silver and gold Kurantgeld, was sufficient to mean that Reichsgeld would only be recognized by the stamp of the Reich. Everywhere the opinion of the coin master prevails, everywhere the view of the autometallism participates. The chartality of money, perceived darkly by practitioners, did not even have a name; one did not differentiate between the price of gold and the price of gold. In short, the theory was in every respect deeply behind the practical action of the practitioner. -

Now is the time to raise the question of why we switched to the gold standard.

Above all, let us note that the transition to a single monetary constitution, and to a constitutional (rather than particular) one, was a very different and much more general issue than that of the transition to the gold standard.

Ever since the Heidelberg Trade Day (1861), it had been envisaged in circles of experts to abolish both the thalers and the southern German guilders, and to introduce in their place the thirds of thaler (the mark) as a unit of value.

At that time, however, one thought only of making this change in such a way that the silver currency remained; nor was it conceivable to dispose of particular legislation from the field of monetary affairs, since there was no Reich constitution. So it should be the hitherto always entered way of coin contracts maintained.

After the establishment of the Reich, the idea emerged victorious that in the future it would be Reichsgeld instead of the Landesgeld. Initially, only the coin money was thought; Later, with the happiest extension of the reform plan, it was added that the cash-notes and, even later, banknotes should also be subject to the Reichsgesetz.

But all this would have been possible within the silver currency as well. So the question is, why did you turn away from the silver and the gold? °

In the sinking of the London silver prices, the reason can not be. In 1871, when the reform began, those silver prices coincidentally stood just as high as the French law of 1803 assumed them to be normal. The sinking began only around 1873 and was at least partly the result of the monetary reforms that were being undertaken at our time and in Scandinavia.

If, in France around the year 1869, the transition to the gold standard was thought of, that was the simple consequence of the constitution in force there, according to which gold had taken the place of silver by itself. In our case, however, where there was no expression of gold, because our constitution before 1871 did not assign gold to the gold, there can be no talk of mere actual penetration of the gold.

The question still remains, therefore, why we have turned to gold, since this step was not necessarily connected with the introduction of a new Reichsgeld.

There was also no elaborate plan for the innovation; neither the government of the Reich nor the then influential publicists surveyed in advance the path to be followed. Only in general did the idea of gold currency emerge. **Soetbeer, a Hamburg publicist, was the most active in the press, full of tireless zeal; and in the Reichstag the deputy**

Bamberger, who, as a connoisseur of the banking industry, enjoyed a high reputation and at important moments made the decision. Bamberger's intervention is already under the influence of the sinking silver prices since 1873, that is, significantly under the influence of a later economic cycle. But what is important to us here is why, before 1871, when silver prices had not yet fallen below those considered normal, the transition to the gold standard was recommended.

The older efforts of Soetbeer and Bamberger (to name only the champions) would be much easier to understand if at that time there had already existed a sound theory of finance and had been called to the aid of those men. That was not the case. What we now present as the theory of finance is all based on experiences made after 1871. It is quite out of the question to conceive of these pioneers as if they had been in the secret possession of the newer theory.
They have created the basis for their actions.
Moreover, Soetbeer was far removed from any theoretical training; Bamberger did not lack the facility, but his practical CV did not allow him to receive any training.

What drove those men back to gambling for gold currency was a dark drive that always underlies acting people. In following this instinct, they often made arguments of great contestability, and it must be said that the weakest reasons made the most impression on the public. The whole reversal in favor of gold nowadays seems to be the result of an instinct that energizes certain bearers and leaders of public opinion: the path they advise in their drive is the way to the right goal; but the reasons why the audience follows them are not always the right reasons.
"Wealthy peoples need money of more precious material than poor peoples." Who does not like to hear that he has become too wealthy to hold on to silver money!

Nevertheless, it is clear and it was then long established that the Dutch are "richer" than we are - and they had kept their silver money, which they had outgrown rather than we.

"Because such large payments, as they have now become frequent, must be made in more handy pieces." This reason, however, refers us to even stronger coercion on banknotes or cash-notes - which also served massively in Germany before 1871 for this purpose. -

- "Then we will be freed from the dangerous paper money" - and, lo and behold, after the introduction of the gold money, we arranged the paper money and, since then, have used it with supreme ease.

"One sees in England that gold always has a fixed value; it is at least doubtful of silver." But it is seen in England, rather, that the so-called firmness of the gold value is a result of the administration of the price of gold, and that, by similar administration, silver might retain or retain this property.

Such and similar reasons, which can not for a moment deceive the connoisseur, are of the highest importance for the so-called public opinion: they have also been victorious; for it is not the goodness of the reason, but its easy complexity in the web of existing wishes that counts. The publicist has to look for reasons that trigger welcome side-conceptions, because the masses are moved by triggering sensations.

If the theorist refers to the utterly inadequate nature of the reasons, the publicist can always reply: I play instruments other than you. I place the soul of my listeners in moods; how I do it, that's my business. But you turn to the mind; may you succeed in controlling him as surely as my hearts will. Six bars of my music are enough to put the listeners in the same step; how long do you need to bring your evidence to life, and how many do you succeed? Can the reform work of public life wait until your evidence works? No. So we publicists work with the mood.

In fact, there are even circumstances in the public that are beyond the scope of any intellectual exercise. As beautiful as the silver is - the gold is more beautiful. The secret coloristic appeal of this metal attracts people. There is something good about seeing gold coins in the English merchant's bag. If only we were that far, thinks the German; and the sideline of English industry and commerce is involuntary.

The real reasons from which the leading spirits were led at that time may well have been the following: If the German Reich at last mends the improving hand, it can not be done thoroughly enough, since such a moment never returns. With bold attempts, however, one likes to lean on proven patterns.   Of the neighbors, however, France had a well-ordered monetary constitution; but it was hardly probable that, after the peace of 1871, Germany would follow the example of France.   All that remained was England; At that time all liberals looked there and besides all hamburger. England's money constitution was well established, so they imitated her. Since England "dominated the world market," Germany at the same time joined in with the monetary system of the world market-a turn which again sounded very promising; and so it was the given thing to rearrange our monetary constitution on the basis of the English model, especially since the procurement of gold was very easy for us because of the then received contribution.

In the course of the reform, Bamberger drew particular attention to the advantage that it has for us that now fluctuations in the exchange rate, for reasons of falling silver prices, between England and Germany are no longer to be feared. In terms of trade policy, the reform was therefore very welcome, as steady exchange rates are generally welcome.
Also, this is the reason for the further expansion of the gold standard after that time - but we could not say anything about that in 1871.
In short, in 1871, it was actually less about the gold itself, but rather about the imitation of the established in England institution. For reasons

of understandable caution, it is better to praise the dead gold than living England under such circumstances. However, it does not follow from all this that we have better remained with the silver or converted to bimetallism, but it follows only that the reasons which have most favored that transition among the great public have very little or no reliability. The real reason has certainly been the connection with the pattern of England, and by going over to this side, the Anschluss also became advisable and, in the end, inevitable for the neighboring states. All this, to say it again, not because gold is gold - but because England is England. -

In the German Reich one always wanted to give the value of the cash in cash, in gold; but how this was done there was uncertainty about it, and so it happened that from 1871 until about 1875 or 1876, we were unaware of the notional constitution of valutary money; Of course, the plates of this money were of silver: no one noticed the fact that our taler money had fallen; and yet argyrodromia had ceased and chrysodromia not yet begun: but all this eluded the sensory observation. It was not until 1876 that the long-sought gold standard was in progress.

Now, as is well known, all of our so many accessory types of money are necessary: all notes are there, and all our coins, except the gold coins, are, and above all, there are also the thalers. In internal traffic, then, the accessory emergency money has the most tremendous spread, so that even with us the valutary cash money is more and more used for exodromic use, just as in England and France.

§ 18c. German Empire; Third party cover 1907

Here and there, for example in the month of October 1906, the German Reichsbank has increased the discount rate to 600. All the newspapers dealt with this event and endeavored to clarify the economic reasons,

reasons that lie in the so-called financial needs of the industry, in the stock exchange and in the customs of the Reich Treasury.

First of all, it must be remembered that the Reichsbank is sometimes urged to increase the rate for discounting bills for two very different reasons: on the one hand, because of industrial recovery; on the other hand, because of the rise of foreign exchange rates. To explain this in a few words, we note above all that the Reichsbank is legally compelled and absolutely determined to carry out the so-called third-party coverage of the issued banknotes: the bank must keep in its coffers the third part of the amount of the issued notes in others money types and in gold bars; By doing so it is considered sufficiently certain that the notes in circulation can be redeemed on demand, to which the bank is obliged.

This third-party coverage is now sometimes in jeopardy in two ways:

1. Suppose that the economic development gives rise to far more changes than before; then much more of these bills will be submitted for discounting, and accordingly more banknotes will come into circulation. As a result - if the supply of those covering money types does not change - the third-party cover can easily be endangered. **To counteract this, the bank increases the discount rate**, thereby preventing an increase in the number of notes issued, while many notes return to the Reichsbank in the course of the next few weeks, depending on the maturity of the bills. The disturbing circumstances with regard to third-party cover are thus eliminated, which, of course, **the merchants and industrialists feel a severe distress**- but viewed from the bank, the desired success, namely pausing the cover rule, enters.

2. But even in a very different situation, the bank increases the discount rate. Let us assume that there is no particular upswing in industry; the resulting bills are no higher in number and amount than usual.

On the other hand, there is a clear prospect of a rise in the price of foreign means of payment: higher prices for the Sovereign and the golden 20 frank coin; above all, higher prices of bills payable in England, France and other neighboring countries. The money changers foresee that the "gold point" will soon enter, that is, such a high rate of foreign currency that it is rewarding to send gold coins abroad. Then the money changers want to have gold pieces at hand; So they submit notes to the Reichsbank for redemption and get really gold pieces, because the Reichsbank voluntarily avoids the presentation of thalers. So the supply of gold pieces in the Reichsbank is decreasing; the third party cover is in danger and to reduce this risk, **the Reichsbank increases the discount rate**, so that fewer notes come into circulation. This will bring the threatened relationship between the circulating notes and the cover funds back in order.

These two cases are not mutually exclusive; It is conceivable that the upswing of the industry at home and the rising course of foreign currency will come together. The prescribed third-party coverage of the notes is then threatened from two sides, so there are two reasons for the discount increase.

It should be noted that the Reichsbank takes its decision not because it can no longer redeem the notes, but because the prescribed third-party cover is in jeopardy; so far, we have only considered the effect of economic cycles and foreign exchange rates. -

But there would also be other considerations in the spot, which are closer to the representatives of the state theory of money than to the economists. Does it depend solely on the operations that are carried out with the money? Or does not the constitution of the money itself have to be examined, that is to say, are not the laws, ordinances, and ordinances, which legally regulate our payment system, certain

reasons which cause here and there such increases in discounts by putting third-party coverage at risk?

Money appears to the public as naturally as language; just as little the layman, when he speaks, thinks of grammar, so little does he think, when he pays, of the constitution of money, which is, so to speak, the grammar of finance.

What about the resources of the bank, which keeps the necessary supply of funds?

The means of cover are: gold in bars, at 1392 marks the pound fine; and five types of money, namely: German gold pieces; Reichsscheidmünzen of silver; Reichsscheidmünzen of copper and nickel; Thaler; Reichskassenscheine.

Of these five types of money, four are completely ineffective: the two types of minor coins are legally redeemable in gold money; the taler is not, however, but the Reichsbank actually redeems them, without legal compulsion, into gold money, and the Reichskassenscheine are again redeemable by law, and finally in gold money. It is clear that money types that can be redeemed themselves do not provide effective cover for the notes of the Reichsbank, although they are legally counted as cover funds.

Effective cover funds are only: the gold bullion and the German gold pieces.

The question then arises: what resources does the Reichsbank have to hold in its coffers a sufficiently large supply of gold pieces or gold bullion? This stock is constantly being changed by the payment system.

Let's first look at the gold pieces. With each disbursement, which is accomplished by the cash register of the Reichsbank - as far as the payment in gold pieces takes place - the stock diminishes; he increases with each deposit to the Reichsbank. The size of the stock thus depends on this back and forth of payments.

Does the Reichsbank now have any means of regulating the amount of that stock of gold coins?

The answer to this question is certainly startling for many people who do not know our monetary system; it is: no; The Reichsbank has no means of regulating the amount of its gold coin stock.

And why not? Because she is compelled to take seven kinds of money in payment; and because it can be forced to make payments in gold pieces.

Just take the trouble to look a moment closer at the details of our Constitution.

Suppose that a payment had to be made to the Reichsbank; which kind of money may the paying customer use? First, gold of the Reich, because this can not be rejected anywhere; secondly, thalers, because they can not be rejected either. Third, and fourth, our two types of minor coins; the private could reject higher amounts, but the bank can not, because these types are redeemable in gold. Fifth, Reichskassenscheine; the private could reject it, but the bank can not. Sixth, Reichsbank notes, for the bank can never refuse to take their notes in payment; only the private can reject it. Finally, at the end, the Reichsbank must legally accept the notes of the remaining other banks, and if the Reichsbank redeems these foreign notes, it is not sure that they will receive gold money, since thalers are also useable; because only the Reichsbank, not the other banks, has renounced the use of Talers.

So there is no means which allowed the Reichsbank to choose among the seven types of money; she must leave the choice to the customer when it comes to payments to the bank.

But what about the payments the bank makes to its customers?

The customer can not refuse gold money, but he can refuse all other six types of money, and that is: the pieces of the taler, because the bank allows it, since it makes no use of the fact that they are enforceable; The customer only needs to accept the two types of coins in very small amounts, so that there is no point in talking about them. The Reichskassen seem to reject the private customer; as well as the Reichsbank notes; as well as the notes of the other banks.

So the customer, who has to receive payment, can not refuse gold pieces, but he can refuse all other kinds of money. So if he makes use of these rights, he has the power to force the Reichsbank to pay gold.

So the supply of gold in the Reichsbank depends entirely on the behavior of the public; the Reichsbank itself has no influence on it - as far as payment traffic is concerned! Although the Reichsbank knows exactly what to expect in payments today - due to maturing bills, Lombard loans or treasury bills - but she does not know what amount of these payments will go into gold money. The entrance of the gold money is regulated by the behavior of the public.

But the public behaves like this: In quiet times no private person feels the need to withhold large stocks of gold pieces; one is glad to have banknotes or cash-notes. If payments are to be made to the bank, then you choose - in quiet times - gold pieces, just to get rid of them. Then, at that time, gold accumulates at the Reichsbank, but not by an active, but by a suffering behavior of this bank.

However, here and there, on certain dates for wages and salaries, there is a need in the public to have pieces of smaller sums at hand, such as pieces of 20 marks and below; many banknotes, which used to amount to at least 100 marks, may for that reason be offered for redemption; but it does not seem as if the redeemers were just pushing to get gold pieces, because taler pieces and five-mark pieces would be even more useful. The audience's need for smaller chunks does not seem to contribute much to depriving the bank of gold.

But when disturbances of calm occur, for example, when the movement of foreign exchange rates causes the "gold point" to appear soon, then our money changers have in sight an advantageous use of the gold coins. This can not be without effect; Who will pay any gold coins to the bank if he has access to a whole range of equally effective other types of money!

In such times, therefore, the gold pieces come in only sparsely, and because of the necessary third-party coverage then the Reichsbank has to limit their notes - unless it strengthens their holdings of gold pieces by special means, or that they buy gold bullion, yes not on enters the payment channels.

But here begins a certain darkness: one does not see right how the Reichsbank, through its own active behavior, can procure gold pieces.

Of course, the Reichskasse sometimes has to make large payments to the bank, for example, when discounted treasury bills fall due; then pay the kingdom in gold pieces? hardly; because the Reichskasse is led by the Reichsbank, and it should be so then the Giroweg be selected, whereby not a single piece of gold enters into the cash of the bank.

It is not at all clear that there is any payment to be made to the bank in which the bank could certainly count on the performance of gold. And what about other ways?

Does the Reich occasionally give gold as a loan to the bank? Also, nothing is known. The 120 million marks in gold pieces that the Reich keeps as a treasury are not used for such purposes.

Nor does one hear that the Reich would be able to deliver "effective gold" against interest-bearing promissory notes in order to make it available to the Reichsbank.

Or does the purchase of gold in bars help? Here is first to distinguish whether such bars are offered or not. In the case of bid, the bank pays 1392 marks for the pound fine. If, however, the bank acts as a seeker, then of course it must pay the price which the owner of Barren demands. Newly produced gold should almost always be offered to the Bank of England and not reach Berlin, which does not rule out the occasional occurrence of smaller-scale such transactions in Berlin.

But more important than this is the other consideration: the seller of bars receives the price in banknotes; but then, as bearer of redeemable notes, he has the means in his hand to withdraw the gold from the bank. The purchase of gold bullion by the Reichsbank is therefore not a sure means of increasing the existence of the Reichsbank in terms of gold. If, however, the bank buys English bills, and after the maturity comes into circulation, it has used banknotes to buy the bills, and the incoming gold can thus disappear again, as in the previous case, because of the redemption of notes , which is established with us as the highest principle.

The Austro-Hungarian Bank only cashes its notes if it likes them, so it can not be forced to do so, which makes the situation quite different.

The Bank of France does not always redeem its notes in gold, at least not readily; very often it requires that the redeemer deduct a deduction of 2 per mille, in which there is a great protection of the stock of gold; but we do not do this because we do not want the "bonus system".

It would be similar to the bonus system in France if the payment to the bank, if made in gold, would give us a discount - say 2 per mille - then customers would be encouraged to choose gold pieces when making payments to the bank; This would certainly increase the stock of gold by increasing supply, while the French system seeks to make the discharge more difficult.
You could even combine the two measures - but nobody will recommend it, even if the one-sided premium already appears inadmissible.

Certain states, such as Austria, can afford certain types of payments in gold; they are the customs payments; in this case the state has significant reserves of gold, and in Austria these supplies are delivered to the central bank; how this is calculated has no meaning here; Suffice it to say that here the bank has a source for the safe receipt of gold money. No such institution is known to us in the German Reich.

It is far from our proposition to make any suggestions here, as this will be a dangerous start if not experienced business people are consulted. Only one point should be clarified, which is easily overlooked by practitioners, who often lack an overview of the constitution of the financial system. This point is: our Reichsbank has no influence on the kinds of money which one brings to it, but it should always be prepared to pay in gold pieces as soon as the customer demands. It follows that the Reichsbank has no means of determining for itself how large its stock of gold money should be; this supply is soon large, sometimes small, depending on the behavior of the public. But because of the coverage rule, it depends on the size of that stock how many notes the Reichsbank is allowed to issue, so how much change they will discount and how much Lombard loan they can grant. As soon as the coverage ratio is in danger, discounting and lombardization must be made more difficult.

Is not there a gap in our bank constitution here? And how is this imperfection explained?

Obviously because our practitioners have no clear idea of the circumstances of our payment system. They only see all sorts of money side by side, coins and bills, and they do not want to know how to use them differently from the rules that have so to speak developed blindly. Our gold standard appears to them as an automaton, which therefore remains on its own; but it is a machine that must be obtained by expert hand. Therefore, the Reichsbank is quite right when it comes to means to regulate their gold reserves, so that they are not disturbed by all sorts of coincidences to fulfill their task.

Should sacrifices be made under certain conditions, the Reich must decide to bring them; under other economic conditions will then find opportunity for a refund.

However, if one sticks to the usual practice, occasionally such discount rates will occur again and again as they were perceived in 1906 as a serious disturbance.

§ 18 d. German Empire 1905 to 1914

I. The Money Constitution at the end of July 1914.

Following the description of the seven money types given above (§ 18a), the changes are to be enumerated here very briefly, according to the order maintained there.

1. Nothing has changed with regard to gold coins; in the newly revised Münzgesetze of June 1, 1909, however, the term "crown" for the ten-mark piece and "double crown" for the twenty-mark piece is no longer used.

2. The Reichsilbermünzen; by law of May 19, 1908, a 3-mark piece is created; the specific content and the rules for use in numbers are fully in line with the rules on 5, 2, 1 and 1/2 marks.

3. Nothing has changed in nickel and copper coins.

4. The one-taler pieces of German character (from the Zollvereinsstaaten) came out of validity, from 1 October 1907; this is the last remnant of thaler pieces; So now all the taler pieces are out of course.

5. **The Reich treasury notes; formerly they were pieced together: 50 Mk., 20 Mk., 5 Mk. By law of June 5, 1906 this is abolished and the new denomination enters into 10 Mk. and 5 Mk. -**

6. The notes of the Reichsbank; earlier they were pieced together: 1,000 Mk.; 100 Mk. By law of February 20, 1906, the Reichsbank is authorized to issue also notes of 50 Mk. And 20 Mk. therefore there are those of 1,000 Marks, 100 Marks, 50 Marks, 20 Marks. By law of June 1, 1909, the Reichsbank is obliged to redeem its notes in German gold coins. Since there are no more thalers since October 1, 1907, and since, moreover, minor coins have to be accepted only up to 20 marks, this provision has hardly any other content than the former: redemption into

"price-capable German money." The only difference is that the single note of 20 marks is not to be redeemed in small coins, but in gold coins. But since the Reichsbank has since 1876 refrained from imposing Talers, nothing has changed in the matter; It would be quite wrong to interpret the law of June 1, 1909, as if the redemption of the Reichsbank notes into German gold money were only then put into action.

Finally, **the notes of the Reichsbank are declared by law of June 1, 1909 as legal tender.** This simplifies the legal situation; but even before that rejections of these notes have hardly occurred. -

7. The notes of the Landesbanks; As long as these notes are redeemed by the issuing body, the Reichsbank has the obligation to exchange the notes of the Landesbanken for Reichsbank notes. -

As regards, finally, the Reich war treasure mentioned above, page 325, it was considerably strengthened by the law of July 3, 1913. 120 million marks are redrafted in silver coins, outside the limit of 20 marks on the head of the population; and also 120 million marks are created in cash (to 10, also to 5 Mk.).
 "The proceeds of these Reich treasury notes are for the procurement of an equal amount in coin gold with the purpose of the Reich war treasure... to use."

By announcement of July 16, 1913, the newly created silver and gold holdings at the Reichsbank for the account of the Reich are "confidently" laid down. -

Almost all the listed changes in our monetary system are insignificant. The Taler had actually disappeared by imprinting in Reich silver coin when they legally lost their validity. The three mark piece is completely irrelevant.

Of some significance is only that **the imperial banknotes are now legal tender**. Thus, the legal situation is as ordered as in England, France and Austria-Hungary, and any uncertainty finally stops.

It is also of great importance that the Reichsbank now uses not only the larger notes (1000 and 100 Mk.) But also smaller pieces (50 and 20 Mk.), And that the Reich treasury notes (Reichskassenscheine) have consistently gone over to the small denomination (10 Mk. And 5 Mk.). -

So it was already taken care of in 1906 to create emergency money of small denominations. As a result, it is no longer necessary to use the gold pieces of 20 Mk. And 10 Mk. Validity in the inner circulation, since you now have small notes at hand. The former principle of avoiding smaller notes is thus abandoned. One does this only when one is convinced that in the internal traffic the emergency money is sufficient - and that our cash money (the gold coins) has to serve for the foreign traffic. **Incidentally, this reason was not cited, but the measure was started without giving a reason.**

A small remnant of imperfection has remained: **the Reichskassen bills have not become legal tender**, while it is the banknotes.

So it was until the month of July 1914: there was only one hylic metal, the gold; the gold coins were the only kind of cash. In addition, there was a lot of emergency money, but all emergency money was redeemable in gold.

The cash money was thus in valutary position. In internal traffic the emergency money was predominant; Although the cash money was also applicable to internal traffic, it was primarily used for foreign trade.

The following overview (pages 358 and 359) gives the condition for the end of July 1914; A similar survey for August 1914 is presented, for easier comparison.

German Empire, end of July 1914.

Deutsches Reich, Ende Juli 1914.

Geldarten	Nach der Einlösbarkeit in Goldmünzen	Nach dem Annahmezwang	Nach der Entstehung	Nach der Zahlweise des Staates
1. Goldmünzen zu 20 u. 10 Mk.	definitiv	Kurantgeld	bares Geld	valutarisch
2. Silbermünzen zu 5, 3, 2, 1, ½ Mk.	einlösbar bei 200 Mk. und mehr	Scheidegeld I	notal	akzessorisch
3. Nickel- u. Kupfermünzen z. 20, 10, 5, 2, 1 Pf.	einlösbar bei 50 Mk. und mehr	Scheidegeld II	notal	akzessorisch
4. Reichskassenscheine zu 10 u. 5 Mk.	einlösbar	fakultativ	notal	akzessorisch
5. Reichsbanknoten zu 1000, 100, 50, 20 Mk.	einlösbar	Kurantgeld	notal	akzessorisch
6. Landesbanknoten z. 100 Mk.	einlösbar	fakultativ	notal	akzessorisch

[Money types
Redemption in gold coins
Acceptance
Payment way (fine gold money, nominal)

By acceptance of the state (valutary, accessory)

1. Gold coins to 20 & 10 Mk. definitely | Kurantgeld cash money | valuta
2. Silver coins redeemable at 5, 3, 2, 1, Mk. and 1/2 Mk until 200 Mk. - notal accessory
3. Nickel and Copper redeemable at coins for 20, 10,5, 2, 1 Pf. - until 50 Mk. I notally accessory
4. Reich Treasury notes to 10 and 5 Mk -redeemable optional notal accessory
5. Reichsbank notes to 1000, 100, 50, 20 Mk. -redeemable cash bonus notary accessory
6. Landesbank notes to 100 Mk redeemable | optional notally accessory]

German Empire, 4th and 31st August 1914.

Deutsches Reich, 4. und 31. August 1914.

Geldarten	Nach der Einlösbarkeit in Goldmünzen	Nach dem Annahmezwang	Nach der Entstehung	Nach der Zahlweise des Staates
1. Goldmünzen zu 20 u. 10 Mk.	definitiv	Kurantgeld	bares Geld	akzessorisch
2. Silbermünzen zu 5, 3, 2, 1 u. ½ Mk.	nicht einlösbar	Scheidegeld I	notal	akzessorisch
3. Nickel- u. Kupfermünzen z. 20, 10, 5, 2, 1 Pf.	nicht einlösbar	Scheidegeld II	notal	akzessorisch
4. Reichskassenscheine zu 10 u. 5 Mk.	nicht einlösbar	Kurantgeld	notal	valutarisch
5. Darlehenskassenscheine zu 50, 20, 10, 5, 2, 1 Mk. (31. Aug.)	nicht einlösbar	fakultativ	notal	akzessorisch
6. Reichsbanknoten zu 1000, 100, 50, 20 Mk.	nicht einlösbar	Kurantgeld	notal	valutarisch
7. Landesbanknoten z. 100 Mk.	nicht einlösbar	fakultativ	notal	akzessorisch

[Money Types Money types
Redemption in gold coins
Acceptance
Payment way (fine gold money, nominal)

By acceptance of the state (valutary, accessory) S° Acceptance Ä Payment way

Gold coins forced the state

1. Gold coins too} - - - - -20 u. 10 Mk. definitely Kurantgeld cash money accessory
2. Silver Coins * * * * - t redeem- to 5, 3, 2, 1 u. not Äös # notal accessory 1/2 Mk. ,
3. Nickel u. Coupling loose - coins for 20, s° # notal accessory 10.5, 2, 1 Pf. S
4. Reich Treasury notes - not redeemable notes to 10 u. not only 5 Mk. -
5. Loan cash vouchers for non-cash - - -
50, 20, 10.5, 2, bar optionally notally accessory 1 Mark (31.Aug.)
6. Reichsbank - 11 / 52- notations to 1000, --- cash amount notional valutary 100, 50.20 Mk.
7. Landesbank- not redeem- optional | notally accessory notenz. 100 Mk. bar]

II. The Constitution of the Monetary System after 4 August 1914.

1. The gold coins are definitely current money as before. But there are no other types of money that are redeemable in gold money.

2. and 3. In the case of silver coins and nickel and copper coins, the solubility in gold money has ceased (for amounts of 200 or 50 Mk.); but they can be redeemed in Reichskassenscheine and in Reichsbank notes.

4. The Reichskassenscheine are no longer redeemable; since they - like the Reichsbank notes - are declared legal tender, they now belong to valutary money.

5. The Loan Cash Vouchers are a new type of cash register of the Reich, because they are accepted in payment at all Reichskassen (as well at all public coffers in all states - probably also in the Reichsland Alsace-Lorraine)

In private traffic a compulsion to accept does not occur; So they are optional money.

They are not redeemable in gold money; nothing is mentioned about it. The purpose is as follows: It was foreseen that many businessmen would feel the need for loans against pledge after the outbreak of the war. Although the Reichsbank manages such transactions, since this institution offers notes to the Lombard customer, and since the notes must be "covered," it would have been necessary to increase the "covering" reserves by means of extended Lombard transactions. Therefore, special loan funds have been set up, which operate Lombard transactions and use for this purpose "Loans", which are not subject to coverage.

6. The Reichsbank notes are no longer redeemable in gold money; since they have general acceptance obligation without redemption, they belong now (like the Reichskassenscheine) to valutary money.

For the cover also loan cash notes are usable, as earlier the Reichskassen seem already (see above P. 327).
The Landesbanken are entitled and obliged to redeem their notes in notes of the Reichsbank. -

The monetary constitution of the German Reich, after the outbreak of the war of 1914, turned out to be this way: Our valutary money has Notalverfassung and consists of the two types: Reichskassen banknotes [like State or treasury notes] and Reichsbank notes, thus from two kinds of paper money.

The gold coins have become accessory money; as such, they can receive and have received a premium. But **since the trade in gold coins is prohibited, agio does not come to light** and is therefore not listed on the stock exchanges.

The expression of gold coins is not set; it could take place, but it does not happen because the private owners of gold bars would not find any benefit.

For the price of the metal gold, the lower limit still remains: one pound of gold can still be converted into 1395 - 3 = 1392 Mk, which gives the lower price limit. However, there is no upper price limit, as our valuta money - those two types of notes - can no longer be redeemed for gold. Chrysodromia has stopped. The gold standard is therefore no longer, because the mere unrestricted expression of the gold is not sufficient. Although gold is still our "hylic" metal, our only one, but this is only a gold-standard device, but in itself does not constitute a gold standard.

It is true that the Reichsbank notes are still covered in accordance with the regulations ("third-party cover", coverage is not required for Reich treasury notes). But the third-party cover has by no means the effect of preventing a Gold agio; only redemption in gold coins would have this effect.

The price of German valutary money on the stock exchanges of foreign countries can only be observed on the stock exchanges of the neutral countries. Earlier, a settlement of this course after the conditions of the coin parities occurred, partly by the redemption of our notes in gold money, partly by exodromic measures of the Reichsbank, since about 1909. These two aids are no longer in progress; the second of these measures may still be minor, but certainly not enough. Therefore, the price of our valutary money is now "anarchic".

The formerly widespread view that the price of our valutary money on the foreign stock exchanges expresses the "confidence" of those countries in our monetary system is now no longer prevalent in the press. For reasons of patriotic mood, this is no longer spoken. At the same time, however, the view has spread that this course depends on the mutual payment conditions, which in our language is nothing other than the insight that this course is defined as "pantopolish." -

Our monetary constitution is now very similar to that which existed in England at the time of the Napoleonic Wars, and in France at the time of the Franco-Prussian War of 1870-71 or in Austria from 1859 to about 1906. In short, it resembles the monetary constitution of all States, which are forced to lead wars, to which the financial strength with "normal" monetary constitution is not sufficient. We have paper money economy!

That may be lamentable, but it is a tremendous tool. No state can do without it under all circumstances. It is not important to complain or condemn them; but it depends on how to heal this condition after peace has come.

To talk about the reorganization after the war has no purpose for the time being; **it must be known beforehand how trade relations with the neighboring states will take shape and whether there will be one among the states that occupies a dominant position. If such a one develops, then the question becomes important, which monetary constitution he will have.**
It is not likely that the German Reich will soon return to the gold standard in the strict sense of the word. Such restorations have always required very long preparations. In France and Italy too, it will hardly happen soon, let alone Russia. For the time being we will stay with the emergency money.

But this does not mean that the Gold is completely deprived of its privileged position in our monetary system.

The assumption of unrestricted currency is likely to remain; In addition, the accumulation of gold reserves will remain with the central banks, as they will presumably continue to be required to regulate the exchange rates. But it is not to be supposed that the unconditional cash redemption of the notes will soon return.

By far the most important question is whether or not the earlier coin-parity phrases between states are retained as rules for the inter-valutary parity.

France and Italy returned to the previous coin parliaments in the 19th century after overcoming their "paper economy"; Russia and Austria, on the other hand, have set up new coin parliaments and have subsequently reorganized the inter-valutary parity.. The ruble, formerly 3,24 Mk., Was reduced to 2,16 Mk. the Austrian Guilder, formerly 2 Mk., to 1.70 Mk.

This is actually the main question that is also playing within our federal cooperative. Will Austria, whose value money on the stock exchange in 1917 is so low compared to the German valutary money, return to the old normal rates (100 kroner = 85 Mk.)? And what will Germany do, which is in a similar situation to the neutral countries?

But it is not our job to talk about the future; only the experiences of the past should be laid down here.

§ 19a. Austria 1857-1892

The Austrian monetary system was rearranged in 1857 and received the constitution which officially bears the name of the "Austrian currency". The term currency is taken in a broader sense to refer to the monetary system at all. According to the opinion at that time, however, it was believed that the reorganization of coinage sufficed; the banknotes were there, of course, and they were irredeemable since 1848, which was considered a great evil - but this means of government money was hoped to be remedied by administrative measures as soon as the new coinage was regulated by law. Therefore, the patent of September 19, 1857 speaks only of coinage, as indeed the German-Austrian Treaty of January 24, 1857 was designated as a coin contract.

From our point of view, that is, in the sense of the Chartal theory, this innovation appears as follows: the imperial state, at that time a unified monarchy, created a new concept of the value unit, the "gulden of the Austrian currency"; by recurrent union this unity was defined as 20/21 of the former unit of value, which was also called Gulden, which we now have to call the older gulden.

Who had to demand 100 older guilders, was now satisfied by 105 "gulden Austrian currency".

The new monetary system was set up in this way: the metal silver was retained as the hylical metal, the only one. From this metal a new form of cash money was made, the guilder piece of Austrian currency; it was, as already apparent from his capacity as cash money, indefinitely out of the pound (500 grams) of fine silver 45 new guilders were coined.

Because of the Synchartal contract with the states of the Zollverein, Vereinstaler were also imprinted, 30 out of the pound of fine silver; this taler was considered, from the Austrian point of view, 1 1/2 gulden of Austrian currency and was also part of the cash money; It has already been mentioned that he had a synchoral position in the association states. but the silver gulden piece of the Austrian currency did not have the synchartal position.

These two types of cash were currant money, and definitely.

The minor coins, which were incorporated into the new monetary system, will be ignored here for the sake of brevity; they were, albeit coins, nominal money.

But there were also emergency moneys: the notes of the Austrian National Bank. This institution, the definitive statutes of which date from 15 July 1817, was the only bank authorized in Austria with the right to issue notes. The circle of their business was strictly limited; essentially, it operated the businesses of discounting bills and loaning on movable pledges (Lombard business).

The Austrian National Bank was allowed to offer notes to customers instead of the then valutary money. The notes were originally instructions on guilders of the Convention foot.

The holder had the right to offer these notes for redemption, whereupon the bank had to pay the amount immediately in gulden of the Convention foot. In private traffic, these notes had no presumption of compulsion, but in epicenter traffic, not only in payments to the bank, which goes without saying, but also in payments to the coffers of the state. These notes had been, then, before 1848, accessory money.

In 1848 it was decreed that the bank was no longer obliged to redeem its notes; but that the epicenter assumption compulsion, as hitherto, persists; that, furthermore, the apocentric and the paracentric assumption of compulsion still occur. These notes were for older guilders, but were replaced in 1857 by notes on gulden of Austrian currency, in such a way that instead of notes of 100 old guilders, 105 gulden appeared in newer notes. These notes, denominated in gulden of Austrian currency, had to be accepted, like the older ones, without exception; So they were, in our sense, emergency moneys; but they were not redeemable - as were the older grades since 1848 - so they were also definite current money, just like the new silver guilder pieces.

There were no purely optional money types.

The system, called the Austrian currency, thus had two types of definitive monetary allowance: first, the new cash money (the new gulden coins and the taler); second, banknotes denominated in gulden of Austrian currency.

The question now is, which definitive currency was valutary. This can not be inferred from the law, but from the administrative order. At first, in 1857, and at the beginning of 1858, the notes of the bank were still unanswerable. It follows that in the said period these banknotes were valutary; the newly created cash money thus had an accessory position; as such, it was able to obtain agio, and this agio had to occur when the silver, used as a plateau, was to be favorably applied, for instance, in the neighboring silver countries of the Zollverein. In fact, the Austrian cash money at that time was premium.

But now it was part of the plan of Austrian reform to restore the redemption of banknotes. The state therefore had to re-equip the bank so far with cash that the bank could redeem the notes in cash on demand. That happened in 1858. After a memorandum on the paper money system, written in k. k. Ministry of Finance, Vienna 1892, page 9, the bank resumed cash payment in the last quarter of 1858; from the 6th of September to the 31st of December, she cashed in 19 million guilders in cash - by nominal value, of course - and thought to proceed in that way - without any fear that all the notes would be presented for redemption ,

As a result, the Austrian cash (Gulden coin and Taler) became valutary. Conceptually it could no longer have a premium, in the sense of the inner silver agio.
But also the inter-valutary agio, against the countries of the Zollverein, judged by the coin exchange rate, had to disappear because of the now

possible automatic regulation of the intervalutary course, as long as not very particularly lengthy pantopolische disturbances occurred. In fact, this benevolent effect was noticeable.

The neighboring changing place Augsburg, located in the Zollverein, showed this immediately after that memorandum. According to coin exchange at par, 100 South German guilders, of which 52 1/2 pieces contained one pound of fine silver, corresponded to almost exactly 85.71 gulden pieces of the Austrian currency; and listed on the Vienna Stock Exchange, the exchange rate on Augsburg:
- on Nov. 29, 1858: 86.60 fl. of Austrian currency
- on Dec. 30, 1858: 85.90 fl. of Austrian currency
so that there was no appreciable deviation from the coin exchange pari any more. Similarly, the exchange rate course against London and against Paris, both judged by the conventional method (note that there was no coin pari against England), was not appreciably different from the coin exchange pari.

With this the Austrian Government had achieved the purpose which it had intended: its currency had cash in silver; the change in currency was restorative; the newly created unit of value "gulden Austrian currency" had for their cash money the advantage of a very simple coin exchange pari to Talers of the Zollvereins (3 such Gulden coin = 2 Taler coins), on which one laid at that time much weight.

Because of the free expression on the one hand and the valutary position of the silver gulden on the other hand, there was also argyrodromia in Austria at that time, fixing the silver price within narrow limits, so that the metallists could enjoy the fixed silver value of the Austrian currency. **In short, everything seemed to be in perfect order, as late as December 31, 1858, when, on the following day, January 1, 1859, the Emperor of France sent a very frosty New**

Year's greeting to the Austrian Ambassador in Paris, and thus the outbreak of war in sight presented.

As in 1848, the state had to reclaim the bank, and from April 1859 the notes were again irrecoverable, with a general compulsory course, so that they entered the position of valutary money. The new cash money, on the other hand, had become accessory again and, as such, was exposed to the emergence of an agio. For the exchange-rate course against the neighboring Zollverein needed, for pantopolish reasons, to become only a little less favorable to Austria than it had been at the end of 1858, so that the Austrian cash money could be sent there favorably; namely the Vereins Taler, because it had direct lytric use in the Zollverein; the silver gulden, on the other hand, because it was there according to a fixed sentence in German valuta money convertible, that is to be attached to the plateau with profit.

According to the "Statistical Tables on the Currency Issue of the Austro-Hungarian Monarchy" Vienna 1892, page 214, the premium on the silver gulden against Austrian paper money on the Vienna Stock Exchange was in percentages:

	Durchschnittlich	Maximum	Minimum
1860	32,32	44,30	24,65
1861	41,25	50,03	35,26
1862	28,07	38,67	17,19
1863	13,79	18,84	10,16
1864	15,72	19,82	13,39
1865	8,32	14,28	5,39

Average ------- maximum | minimum
1860. , , | 32.32 44.30 24.65
1861. , , | 41.25 50.03 35.26
1862. , , | 28.07 38.67 17.19
1863. , , | 13.79 18.84 10.16
1864. , , | 15.72 19.82 13.39
1865. , , , , 8.32 14.28   5.39

This economic situation, and with it that agio, thus came and lasted several years, because it was not until the end of 1865 that the situation which the unfavorable war in Lombardy had created in 1859 had almost been overcome, and it was hoped that the "production of the currency" would soon be established ,

But that is according to the former opinion, translated into our language: the cash of the Austrian currency should be valutary again, the banknotes again accessory.

Then the much-vowed agio would immediately disappear again.

Now the year 1866 appeared with the Prussian-Austrian war, whose description does not belong here. Despite best intentions, the state could not help but force help from the bank again. He did it by creating state notes or, as even the memorandum of the Ministry of Finance "On the course of the currency issue since 1867" (Vienna 1892, page 34) expresses himself: the state set the printing press in motion. A lot of respect does not betray this expression. It is well known that major political accidents leave behind a mood of indifference that is aimed at individuals, even at things. The state notes have been the creature of the greatest need, so they are hateful, and they do not like to be mentioned as a means of restoration.

Very strange was the beginning of this development. At that time the banknotes were in such a way divided: 1 fl., 5fl., 10 fl., 100 fl., 1,000 guilders. Now the law of May 5, 1866, appeared, demanding that the Austrian National Bank grant a loan to the State, payable in banknotes of ten fl., One hundred fl., Or one thousand fl. The amount of this loan should be as large as the amount of circulating notes at 1 fl. and at 5 fl .; and, in return for offering the National Bank, the state declared that from now on, the small notes (1 fl and 5 fl.) should no longer be banknotes but **state notes**. (Memorandum, page 34.)

Since we do not attach any importance to the inscription on such notes, the understanding has no difficulty: the small "banknotes" were now released from their connection with the bank; the state explicitly stated that it no longer regarded them as promissory notes of the bank, now or in the future.

But these bills are now recognized as promissory notes of the state; not as if the state were ready to redeem it: that is explicitly rejected. The new state grade is just as impossible redeemable as it was the banknote. There is only the political possibility that the redemption will be revived, not by the bank, but by the state. For the time being, the state is only prepared to accept payments in its notes, that is, to compensate for what it owes to it - on a given occasion - by what it owes the customer. **This is the position of the state note in the financial law of the states.** Added to this is the position in the Charter Law, where the state note is treated just like the banknotes that persist, that is, the state uses it apocentrically, and it also gives them general compulsory course.

A little later, the state has given a new form to the notes it took over (which still bore the name of the bank); he has put "formal" notes of the state in its place, and when he saw himself compelled to create state notes, he always created those which were also identified in the inscription as **notes of the state**. This went on until December 1867, when **it was decided that the sum of 312 million guilders in the meantime reached by the state could no longer be crossed**. In addition, the banknotes remained unchanged in their constitution.

Externally, these two types of notes were also clearly distinguishable from the fact that the government notes are differently divided (1 fl., 5 fl., 25 fl., 50 fl.) Than the banknotes (10 fl., 100 fl., 1,000 fl.).

From May, 1866 onward, there are two types of indissoluble notes in Austria: those of the bank, namely those issued by the bank; and **those issued by the state**. Both genera are **at the same time, by the special provisions of the laws, state money**. It should be noted that this does not follow from the concept of banknotes, but is a secondary property. For the state notes, the epicenter assumption follows from the term. In any case, the legislation has ensured that **both types of notes are really Austrian state money** (and also the silver gulden this property remains because he was not de-chartered). -

Which of these money types is valutary, which, however, accessory?

If we refer to the end of the year 1866, the silver gulden was still accessory.
Valutary were and remained the banknotes.
And the newly created government notes were also valuta.

From then on, there were two types of valutary money - while we used to say prematurely that there could be only one currency type.

But there were only apparently two valutary types of money; in fact, as you can see, there was only one, and this was the totality of the notes, namely banknotes and state notes, as an undifferentiated mass. Thus, in total, the marks from 1866 onwards are valutary money, despite political and textual differences, and this is because the state has declared:

If I do not have to pay through special contracts in silver gulden (as in the interest on certain bonds), then I reserve the right to pay either in government notes or in banknotes at my discretion.

In this unquestionable legal exercise it is stated that the notes are without doubt valutary money. It is still possible to distinguish them into banknotes and national notes, but only according to features which are of no significance for the present question.

So from 1866 onwards we have the marks (no matter what origin) as valuta money; and as accessory money the silver gulden together with the taler with bar constitution.

This constitution did not change until 1879, but the course of valutary Austrian money was raised against foreign countries, especially against Germany.

As always, this was due to pantopolish reasons and must by no means be attributed solely to metallopolic causes, although, as we know, metal trade of all kinds is included in the pantopolis.

The general conditions were something like this:
The Italian war in 1859 had already shattered the finances of Austria in the beginning; the unfortunate outcome did not improve the situation. The tax power of the monarchy was low, the deficit in the budget of the state became a standing phenomenon. Bonds did not want to succeed either domestically or abroad, because everyone knew the weak position of the Treasury.

On the other hand, private employment in Austria was low; apart from Bohemia, the empire was entirely agrarian; Freedom of trade, first introduced in 1859 as a result of defeat, could only gradually lead to greater industrial development.

At that time, the Reich essentially exported industrial products, agricultural products. The Treasury was indebted to foreign countries, especially southern and western Germany.

Under such circumstances, which are only briefly indicated, we need to explain how the exchange rate did occurs: Austrian money was little sought after on the stock market compared to German money - and the gulden in notes was therefore no longer on the stock market to 2/3 taler to install, but far less. Also, nobody was able - neither bank nor state - to counter this result of the judgment of **the stock exchange people**.

Since 1866 Austria has experienced only one military activity, the occupation of Bosnia and Herzegovina, a campaign of minor importance. Internal turmoil was not lacking, but warlike suppression of unrest was no longer a cause. Trade and industry rose year by year. The tax capacity of the inhabitants increased, the deficit in the national budgets was reduced and disappeared. Austrian bonds, as good as impracticable in 1866, were smoothly housed abroad. The reluctance of foreign countries to enter into business relations with Austrian entrepreneurs was diminished, Austria also found sales for its goods in the western and northern neighboring states.

After all that is said often enough, the exchange rate, which, if it lacks the exodromic late aid, is nothing more than the result of such circumstances on the stock market, which is determined by the decisions of the exchange visitors to one unite numerical expressions.

In spite of all the improvement of the course against Germany, one thing must not be forgotten: despite all this, the course level which would have corresponded to the coin pari of 1857 was not reached again; never again was the Austrian guilder paid (in value currency, that is, in notes) on the Berlin stock exchange with 2/3 thalers, but it stood lower; and never was the taler on the stock exchange in Vienna for 1 1/2 Austrian guilders (valutary money, so in notes) to have, but it stood higher. And so it was not only until 1871, but from there on to the present. The fact that the mark was set up as a single unit in Germany in

1871 and had a gold standard from 1876 onwards is quite indifferent to the question at hand here, because it only changes the word by saying that the Austrian guilder was in Berlin always lower than 2 marks; in Vienna, the mark was always higher than 1/3 times 1 1/2 gulden. So it is that course, which would have corresponded to the coin pari of 1857, never reentered; always the course was less favorable for Austria. To begin with, in 1892 the Austrian gulden in Berlin was paid at about 1.70 marks (instead of 2 marks), and this stand had set up without any artificial intervention, and thus corresponded to the then pantopolish circumstances, that of No exodromic administration were directed, but seemed anarchic, so to speak.

The course of the silver taler piece in Vienna now easily adjoined to this course of the exchange-rate course, because this piece was synchartal, that is, because it could be used directly for payments to Germany; this applies to all the thaler pieces, including the Vereinstaler Austrian features, which occupy us alone at the moment. Although this would be Taler coin, because it was accessory in Austria, also able to show a Platonic Agio (for reasons of silver price in London); but since this platonic agio, after the fall in the price of silver, was not so high as the inter-valutary agio, which rested on syncharchy, it remained ineffective, and only the inter-valutary agio emerged for the thaler, and persisted until the Austrian club-thaler ceased to be Austrian money (June 1, 1893). From this point on it does not interest us any further; so that we need not mention here that the Austrian Vereinstaler lost its validity in Germany only at the end of the year 1900.

Hereby the agio of a kind of the Austrian cash money, namely the Austrian Vereinstalers, is settled.

The other kind of cash, the Austrian silver gulden, had quite different fates with regard to agio. First of all, the time before 1871 was to be considered when argyrolepsy existed in Germany. Since the silver gulden could be shipped to Germany and converted there in Taler. The costs are low and should be ignored here. As a result of this possibility, the course of the silver gulden in Vienna was almost the same as the course of the thaler in Vienna, but not for reasons of synculature but for argyroleptic reasons.

But when in 1871 argyrolepsia ceased in Germany, the course of the silver gulden in Vienna depended on very different circumstances: its fate differed from that of the Austrian taler, for although both types of coin were technically so closely related, they were legally quite different Personality: the Synchartismus stuck only to the thaler, but not the gulden piece. For this last piece, it was only possible to consider whether it could receive or retain a metallopolic premium, as accessory Austrian money; and for that the conditions on the London silver market were decisive, in connection with the Austrian-English intervalutary courses.

The London silver price, as we know, depends not only on the silver production and consumption of this metal, but also on England's exchange-rate courses against all the countries which still have argyrolepsia; but Austria is among them until 1879, but this state is only one of many, so that the London Silver Prize - we must not say completely independent, but we may say: is not solely dependent on the Anglo-Austrian intervalutary rate.

On the other hand, the Anglo-Austrian intervalutary rate is not completely independent of the silver trade between Austria and England, but this trade plays only a subordinate role, and that price is not, in any case, solely dependent on that silver trade.

Accordingly, the two phenomena, namely, on the one hand, the London silver price and, on the other hand, the English-Austrian exchange-rate course, are not readily derivable, but are essentially independent of each other, despite some subordinate influences existing between them. It is very important to record this, because that is the basis for considering both phenomena as though they were independent of one another; they are only in the main, but that is enough.

From 1871 on the agio - positive as well as negative - of the silver gulden in Vienna depends on the following metallopolic circumstances, whereby we refrain from transport costs and fees:

1. What does the ounce of standard silver in London, expressed in pence, cost in 1/240 pounds sterling? It is easy to deduce how much sterling is given there for a metric pound of fine silver; in every 45 silver gulden (apart from the wear) one metric pound of fine silver is contained; The price of 45 silver coins each, which can be obtained in London, expressed in pounds sterling, is therefore easy to calculate.

2. But whether this sale is advantageous then depends further on the Austro-English exchange rate: that price, say x £ sterling, must, according to the rate of the day, be converted into Austrian valuta money (ie notes), more than 45 Guilders in notes amount. Then the sale is advantageous. But if just 45 gulden in notes could be achieved, would take place balance - that trade would be omitted for lack of profit. But if less than 45 guilders would be achieved in notes, then not only stop that trade, because of imminent loss, but the economy reverses: then it is rewarding to buy silver in London, bring this metal to Austria and to have it coined in silver gulden (which was permitted until 1879), because these silver gulden are indeed accessory money, but they are currency money: one can make any payment with it.

It therefore depends on a certain ratio of the London silver price to the simultaneous exchange rate course of the countries England and Austria, whether the silver gulden a positive premium (in the first cycle) or zero premium (in the second cycle) or a negative premium (at the third economy), whereby the Austrian valutary money forms the point of comparison. Nothing is easier to understand than this, once the concept of metallopolic agios has been obtained. But nobody was prepared for this consideration in Austria. The agioteurs also expected that the metallopolic agio of the silver gulden would remain positive, as it had been since 1859. For no one could foresee that (as from 1876 onwards) the price of silver would be so deep, and at the same time that the Austro-British intervalutarian rate would be as high as it first occurred in 1878.

In the Statistical Tables on the Currency Issue of the Austro-Hungarian Monarchy, Vienna, 1892, page 221, Table 145, the following is found:

Ende des Monats	In Wien Vistakurs London 10 Pfd. Sterling in Gulden ö. W.		In London Silberpreis per Unze Standard in Pence Sterling	100 fl. Silber von London nach Wien kalkulieren ohne Spesen	
	fl.	kr.		fl.	kr.
1878 Januar . .	119	39	53⁷/₈	103	50
Februar . .	120	20	55	106	38
März . . .	122	92	54⁵/₈	108	05
April . . .	123	67	53³/₄	106	96
Mai . . .	119	39	53⁵/₁₆	102	42
Juni . . .	117	22	52³/₄	99	50
Juli . . .	115	60	52³/₄	98	12
August . .	116	54	52¹/₈	97	75
September .	117	55	51⁵/₈	97	65
Oktober . .	119	11	50¹/₂	96	79
November .	117	80	50³/₄	96	20
Dezember .	118	51	49⁵/₈	94	63
1879 Januar . .	117	47	50	94	51
Februar . .	117	47	49⁵/₈	93	80
März . . .	117	58	49¹/₂	93	66
April . . .	117	59	50¹/₈	94	85
Mai . . .	117	03	51¹/₄	96	51
Juni . . .	116	58	52¹/₈	97	78
Juli . . .	116	33	51¹/₈	95	70
August . .	118	24	51³/₈	97	75
September .	117	38	51⁴/₁₆	97	39
Oktober . .	116	88	53⁴/₁₆	100	74
November .	117	42	53³/₁₆	100	26
Dezember .	117	68	52⁷/₁₆	99	30

Nach der Formel: Vistakurs London in Wien multipliziert mit Silberpreis per Unze Standard in London, dividiert durch die Verhältniszahl 62,145, welche daraus folgt, daß 45 fl. Silber 500 Gramm fein, 373,242 Gramm 1 Troypfund, 1 Troypfund 12 Unzen, 37 Unzen fein 40 Unzen Standard, 240 Pence 1 Pfund Sterling.

[End of the month
In Vienna Vistakurs London 10 lbs sterling in gulden
In London silver price per ounce standard in pence sterling
100 fl. Silver from London to Vienna calculate without expenses

fl. kr. fl. kr.
1878 January. , 119 39 537/8 103 50
February. , 120 20 55 106 38
March . , , 122 92 548/8 108 05
April . , , 123 67 533/4 106 96
May. , , | 119 | 39 535/16 102 42
June. , 117 22 523/4 99 50

July 115 60 523/4 98 12
August. , 116 54 521/8 97 75
September. | 117 55 5158 97 65
October. 119 | 11 501/2 96 79
November. 117 80 50 ° / 4 96 20
December . | 118 51 49% / s 94 63
1879 January. , 117 47 50 94 51
February. , | 117 47 4958 93 80
March . , , 117 58 491/2 93 66
April . , , 117 59 501/8 94 85
May. , 117 03 511/4 96 51
June. , , 116 58 521/8 97 | 78
July 116 33 511/8 95 70
August. , | 118 24 518/8 97 75
September. | 117 38 514/16 97 39
October. 116 88 53 * / 16 100 74
November. 117 42 531/16 100 26
December 117 68 527/16 99 | 30

By the formula: Vistaturs London in Vienna multiplied by the silver price per ounce standard in London, divided by the ratio 62,145, which implies that 45fl. Silver 500 grams fine, 373.242 grams 1 troy pound, 1 troy pound and 12 ounces, 37 ounces fine 40 ounces standard, 240 pence 1 pound sterling.]

Let us take this time, at the end of June, 1878. In London at that time the ounce of standard silver cost 52 3/4 pence; and in Vienna, for £ 10 sterling, 117.22 guilders of Austrian currency were then paid in notes. Whoever wanted to sell 100 silver gulden as a commodity in London under these circumstances achieved 99.50 gulden of Austrian currency in notes - in other words, he had no profit, but even an insignificant loss. Therefore, an agio of the silver gulden was no longer possible.

The result for Austria was as follows: private persons in possession of silver guldens could use them, as usual, for payments, and now without them acting unwise, for there was no other use more advantageous would have been. The same is true of the bank; and also from the state. As a result, it happened, and often enough, that silver gulden appeared again in traffic, which had not been seen before June 1878.

Is this, as is often said, a regulation of the Austrian currency within the meaning of the legislation of 1857? No! Only the agony of the silver gulden has disappeared, there can be no doubt about that. Conditions have also arisen that would have greatly facilitated the restoration of the Austrian currency within the meaning of the legislation of 1857; but these relations are not in themselves synonymous with that restoration.

The difference can easily be made clear. In 1857, the goal was that the then new silver gulden should be valutary money, but the valutary position of the silver gulden had stopped again since 1859.

After this, the agony of the silver gulden had occurred, because of the combined effect of the London silver price and the Austro-English exchange rate. When, in June, 1878, this combined effect no longer allowed any agony of the silver gulden, the agio had vanished-but the silver gulden had not regained its value as valuta. For the Austrian State by no means declared that it was prepared to use the silver gulden as a last resort in apocentric payments. Rather, he stuck to his habit of paying in notes (be its banknotes or national notes). The state only reserved the right to occasionally, if it pleased him, offer silver gulden, which, however, could not be rejected, as they had not previously been refused.

Furthermore, the notes remained legally irresolvable; neither was the state obliged to redeem its government notes in silver gulden, nor was the bank obliged to redeem the banknotes in silver gulden.

In other words, the two types of notes, considered as a whole, remained valued money even after June 1878. The silver gulden, on the other hand, remained accessory money even after this time; only they had no platysical overvaluation, but their plate value was equal to their validity and was soon even slightly lower than their validity, so they went to the plateau equivalency to get after some time even Platische sub-valency.

These changes in the Platonic behavior are not the same as the transition from the accessory position to the valutary position. Platic overvaluation, equivalency and sub valency depend on silver prices and exchange rates, that is, on economic phenomena that appear on the stock market. On the other hand, the transition from the accessory position of the silver gulden to the valutary position depends on a decision of the state as to which kind of money he would like to use as a last resort in apocentric payments.

But this decision is an act of politics, be it legislation or administrative practice. It is not the stock market that matters here, but the state power. The state, however, can consider the events on the stock market and then take its decisions. But he has yet to make such a decision - and the Austrian state has not done that! In this omission it is quite clear that the state no longer regarded the "establishment of the currency" or the "regulation of the currency" in the sense of the legislation of 1857 as a political goal. -

Anyone who saw it as the evil of the Austrian constitution, that since the beginning of 1859 the silver gulden had had a premium, had to judge: the evil was healed.

Thus, as Karl Menger (The Value Regulation in Austria-Hungary, Yearbooks of Economics and Statistics, Third Series, Volume 3, 1892) stresses, one should expect that the stock exchange in Vienna would be overly excited about the unexpected by no intentional induced turn. Oddly enough, the fact made little impression. The stock market, completely devoid of anything in theoretical matters, but also without any pretensions, is in practical terms of a certain infallibility: it is rarely mistaken, because the people who go there are thinking about nothing but their interest. The disappearance of the agony of the silver gulden did not cause any particular joy: apparently because the stock market people did not recognize any promotion of their interests. Also in the Ministry of Finance was no particular excitement to notice.

In this process, contrary to previous assumptions, it no longer seemed to rest on the expected salvation.

The state first let things go, and from this a very strange situation developed.

Those business men who used to sell silver gulves as a commodity when silver gulden still existed as silver, bought silver in London, and let it come to Vienna, since it would not cost 45 pounds for a pound of silver, but perhaps only forty-two gulden had to spend even less in notes.

This cheaply acquired silver could now be used with advantage in Vienna: either by having it coined, with 45 gulden in silver for it; or by handing it over to the bank, which had to give it 45 gulden in notes, by virtue of a statutory provision. The business profit of the agioteure achieved in this way is quite incontestable; it was also conceivable that the economic cycle that made this speculation possible would take a long time, because London's silver prices were plummeting, and the exchange rate did not change in a compensatory sense. In short, while in former times the silver guldens rolled out of Austria to be sold in London as plates, now the silver bars came to London from Austria, to be turned into Austrian money there, as this was still legally possible in Austria at certain rates. A legitimate business - but maybe a bad business!

In fact, it soon became apparent that this business - the provisionally unlimited importation of cheaply purchased silver, which could always be converted into Austrian money at the rate of £ 45 per pound - was damaging. The representatives of quantity theory justified this in such a way: the supplies of Austrian money increase now again, as it had happened since 1866 by the creation of the state notes. Therefore, sooner or later the exchange rate will change unfavorably, that is, more florins will have to be given in notes for 10 pounds sterling than before. The Austrian money will suffer, compared to the English, a loss to the course. Therefore, that business of the agioteure, although permitted by civil law, is obviously against the public interest.

Who, on the other hand, does not share this conception, could say so: that the silver is brought in with great advantage for the agioteur, the consequence is that these businessmen constantly seek to acquire English means of payment on the highest scale against Austrian notes; they therefore decide, within the limits of the advantages, to offer more Austrian guilders for the pound sterling than hitherto.
So here's a circumstance that depresses the price of the notes against English money. Note that this is not the amount of Austrian money per se, but the incentive to raise English money.

However, one or the other view may be brought in: in this the evaluations agree that that business of the agioteurs depresses the course of the Austrian notes against the English money, and if one sees therein a loss for the Austrian state, then a whole results strange, hitherto hidden judgment on the Austrian monetary system. Namely: as politically desirable does not appear (as had been believed until 1871, perhaps even longer) the restoration of the lost silver currency. But the politically correct goal is: Preventing the sinking of the Austrian currency against England. Just consider what an incredible turnaround of intuitions lies in it! In 1857 it was said that our monetary system was supposed to be the silver currency, and when this condition did not last, the paper money economy was lamented, on the ground that the good, good silver gulden had an agio. The evil, then, seemed to lie in the lost paragon of the silver gulden.

Now, in 1878, the paragon of the silver gulden (with the notes) returns - and they pay no attention to it.

Furthermore, the silver currency would have been very easy to restore at that time, and it was not.

It follows quite plainly that in 1857 the silver currency was not introduced because silver is silver; but because of the silver currency in Germany. In 1878 the return to the silver currency is dropped because in Germany and England the gold standard now exists. All that is felt now is an evil that depresses the price of Austrian notes against the countries with gold currency.

So what does Austria want?

Not the production of the silver currency, that is, not the return to the metal from which one started in 1857. But solid ratio, at least not a sinking of the notes against the money of the western neighbors. But in the West you have gold currency. So you want a firm relationship, at least no sinking, the Austrian notes against gold. Maybe because gold is gold? Not at all; but because Western neighbors now have gold currency.

The whole behavior of the Austrian state since 1878 (more since 1892) reveals this reversal. One generally thinks of valutary cash. But the choice of metal depends on the facilities of the most important neighbors.

Only the economically most independent state chooses the metal at will. The weaker states follow him, not because they are interested in metals, but in the strength of the exchange rate. The metal is therefore a minor matter. The main thing is the exchange rate. From this, however, it is sufficiently clear what the state decided: its policy was guided by the fight against that danger.

This policy initially consisted of an omission. It was omitted to raise the silver gulden for valutary money and thus to return to the condition of 1858. Second, however, one proceeded to eliminate the danger which resulted from the then profitable silver purchases of the agioteurs; it does not matter whether the danger has been realized or not, and it does not matter how it was founded. It is enough to believe in the danger.

The measure to which it was decided was known as follows:
In January 1879, the Austrian mints were instructed not to accept silver for redemption if it was given by private persons or by the bank. So the earlier stipulation that every pound of silver that was given was to be redeemed with 45 silver coins was lifted. That older provision was based on a law; **the change was not based on a law but on a ministerial decree**. This may be very strange in terms of constitutional law - but for the Chartal Law the difference is without any significance. This removed what in Austria corresponds to the so-called free expression of silver.

Of course, in the interest of the bank, too, the other provision had to be made: the bank was relieved of the obligation to accept silver, the pound of 45 gulden in banknotes - otherwise the silver would have been delivered to the bank, but it would have been delivered because of the previously considered Determination would not have been more pronounced, more correctly: not in silver gulden could have exchanged.

This put an end to speculation, which had been advantageous since June, 1878; if there was a danger in it, that danger was now eliminated. From this side, no adverse effect on the Austrian currency was more to be feared. - -

One circumstance is still to be mentioned: the so-called "silver" of the Empire. **The Austrian state derives a lot of silver from its fiscal (Hungarian) mines, which it does not buy, but for which it only spends the production costs.** Of course, this silver was always pronounced silver gulden; and the state continued to do so, even after January 1879, when the so-called free status for private individuals (and for the bank) was discontinued. "Only silver mines won in Austria and Hungary, but partly also broken silver by the mints, was pronounced". It was from the beginning of 1880 until the complete cessation of silver embossing on October 21, 1892:

in Austria:	in Hungary:	together:
fl. 69 228 894	fl. 44 143 418	fl.113 372 312.

(See [Friedrich Schmid] Die Agioreferve der öfterreichifch-ungarifchen Bank, Wien bei Hölder, 1898, page 59.)

It has been declared a mistake that the attitude was not earlier, about 1879, done; but this is only an error in the sense of quantity theory; On the other hand, in our sense it was only wrong to be determined to transfer to the gold standard in 1879, to the exclusion of silver emergency money - and that was not one. -

The most peculiar consequence of the measure of 1879, according to which no more silver, when supplied by private persons, was turned into money, must still be called by the true name: its effect was that the existing supplies of silver gulden, as well as the new growth of foreign Metal, stopped being cash money! Of course, they did not stop to have silver plates. Also, silver continued to be a precious metal in the technical sense. But the silver was no longer hylic metal, and at that moment the silver gulden were turning into emergency money. The State had reserved the money for this emergency money, occasionally made of Hungarian silver, while in 1867 he had solemnly declared that the emergency money consisting of papery notes of the State had become immeasurable.

But since before 1879, apart from the thalers divisionald from circulation, there had existed only one kind of cash, namely, the silver gulden, after their transformation into emergency money there was no more cash at all, but only a small amount. however, there were many different types among them, namely - apart from the divisional money - both the banknotes and the national notes as finally the silver gulden; but they were necessarily all three in our sense; All three were not hylogenic, even the silver gulden were no longer in our favor, although they had been earlier.

Banknotes and national notes together represented the valutary money; the silver gulden that had become bad were still accessory and now had negative internal agio, as their plates, considered as a commodity, would have been lower in price than they were when used lytrically. So the state had no reason to deny silver gulches in apocentric payments; he occasionally offered them, but he did not offer them as a principal means of payment, and it is because of this that silver money remained accessory. -

Accordingly, the constitution of the monetary system, which bore the name of the "Austrian currency", has undergone the following development:

In the last months of 1858 their currency had the cash constitution with the hylischen metals silver. The accessory money types were all necessary and all had a negative premium; if we ignore the divisional payment, this was negative agio (that of the banknotes, as there were no government notes) as large as possible: it was 100% of the validity.

From the year 1859 to 1878 the valutary money was necessary; the bar constitution of the silver gulden pieces still existed, but this bare money was accessory; it had positive agio of varying altitude, and therefore it stood, practically considered, outside the traffic, although it continued to be public money. This positive agio equaled zero towards the end of 1878, and so the silver gulden returned to circulation, but they remained accessory.

The appearance of government notes in 1866 means only a new kind of emergency money, which put aside the older kind, that is, the banknotes. Lytrically speaking, these two types of papyroplatic emergency expenses do not differ from each other.

From 1879 nothing changes in valuta money, so it remains necessary; on the other hand, the bar constitution of the silver gulden ceases, while their status as state money is not changed; also the silver gulden remain in accessory position; on the other hand, its inner agio becomes negative.

In its last form, the monetary constitution, called the "Austrian currency," has the property that it no longer includes any cash in itself: a barely conceivable strangeness to the metallists, but a very strange one for the proponents of chartal theory; because it does not belong to the essence, but only to the possibilities that it is hylogenic, and therefore that there is orthotypic (cash) money.

In the whole period from 1859 to 1879, however, there is no hylodromia, although the silver is hylic metal; for the silver is convertible into money, but the valutary money is not convertible into silver; Thus, although there is the hyloleptic, but not the hylophantic branch of hylodromic administration. Therefore, the price of silver in Austria was not fixed at that time, whereas in the last months of 1858 it was fixed.

From 1879 until the reform of 1892, hylo-dystonia is also missing, but for another reason: silver had lost its hylic position, and no other metal had become hylic.

All in all, hylodromia is absent from 1859 until the abolition of the "Austrian currency"; consequently, it was only effective during the last months of 1858. -

Quite similar is the case with exodromy; It was only in the last months of 1858, as an automatic regulation of the exchange rate course against the silver countries of the Zollverein, in effect. From 1859 on, however, an automatic effectiveness was impossible because the Austrian valutary money no longer had the cash constitution. It is therefore still to be asked whether, from 1859, there had been a conscious exodromy, for instance through intervention by the bank or another institution, namely a conscious counter-speculation on the stock exchange, about the inter-valutary course against Germany, and for pantopolish reasons for Austria was always unfavorable to lift accordingly. Such an exodromic procedure never existed at that time. The exchange-rate course against Germany always remained anarchic, as we have said above, and was regarded as a fatality; partly because at that time the idea of a deliberate course regulation was still lacking, but partly - and most of all - because the financial weakness of the Austrian state was so great that it seemed quite impossible to provide any institution with such significant reserves of money as they would have been needed to start that deliberate counter-speculation. It would by no means have been necessary to put money into valutary position, although this means would certainly have served the purpose; even the less comprehensive means which we have indicated would have been sufficient - but even then the state perhaps lacked the insight and at least the financial strength.

§ 19 b. - Austria-Hungary 1892 to 1900

The monetary policy of 1857 was so often and so strongly affected by mishap that it only served its purpose for a very short time (late 1858); from then until 1892 it was considered an accident and considered to be in need of reform. But why? We can best deduce this from the measures of reform itself, by imagining the legislator as a consciously acting person, who carries out his criticism of the past not in words but in new creations.

Above all, pay attention to what has been omitted. In 1858, it was possible to regulate the intervalutarian course against Germany so that the German unit of value, called the Taler, and the Austrian, called Gulden, behaved on the stock exchange as if they were 1 1/2 to 1. This level of the inter-valutary rate passed lost in 1859, did not re-enter later, and was not restored by the 1892 reform, nor even sought after. So the goal of the reform was not to re-establish the 1848 inter-party course. Those interested in Germany, especially the owners of Austrian promissory notes, which were interest-bearing in gulden, had perhaps hoped - but their wishes remained unfulfilled. It is not asserted that Austria has violated existing rights because, in our opinion, the foreign creditor of every state, including Austria, must be fooled into being treated like the people in the country - unless he is helped by special conditions Clauses would be protected; and even then that foreign creditor will have no legal means to enforce his claims. So rights were not broken, but hopes were deceived. Austria also did not invoke the statute of limitations of rights, but the limitation of hopes.

The only means by which the foreign creditors could defend themselves was to relieve their confidence in the Austrian state, that is, to decide in the future not to become further creditors of that state; some did it; but many others did not, and preferred to suffer the deterioration of their situation by conceiving a new hope, namely, that in the future at least a further deterioration of their situation would no longer occur. This helpless situation of the creditor of foreign states is a very general phenomenon that is only slightly forgotten because it remains hidden as long as the debtor state does not fall into any serious crises. Also, those creditors want to remain creditors of any state, and separate themselves from the state that has deceived their hopes, only when other states seem to offer better conditions and greater security, which is by no means always the case. Thus it is that the pain of that disappointment is soon overcome: one does not withdraw his trust, because it may be equally unfavorable to turn this trust over to other states.

This should not encourage a breach of trust; it is only to be said how the matter is for the one who confines himself to pure observation. It is well-known how much each state damages its own interests by such breaches of trust; this danger of the reckless state is the only guarantee given to the foreign creditor. -

It is just as clear, on the other hand, that the reform of 1892 wanted to fortify the exchange-rate system against the neighboring countries of the gold standard from now on. So the mobility should stop. But on which state should the attachment relate? Not on a long-forgotten stand, but on the one who had evolved pantopically in the last period before 1892. They considered how to find this estate and decided to conduct the following investigation (ignoring the strange detours as insignificant): How high was the median stand of the Napoleons, that is, the French twenty Franc piece, in the years 1879 to 1891, including at the Vienna Stock Exchange?

From the number found, it was calculated how high the average level of the guilder of Austrian currency had been, expressed in Swiss francs. It turned out that the guilder of Austrian currency, in value currency, had a median value of 2.10 francs. (See statistical tables on currency issues, Vienna 1892, page 239, Table 160.)

The fact that Austria would have to change to the gold standard was already clear among all advisers. It was therefore, according to the example of the western neighboring countries, to create a cash gold money.

It was decided to arrange the new gold coins in such a way that they had, compared to the Napoleon Gate, the coin pari which corresponds to that median value of 1 gulden of Austrian currency equal to 2,10 francs.

Consequently, from the kilogram of fine gold coins of the total value of 3,279 1/9 half guilders had to be minted, for which purpose one set for simplification: the kilogram of fine gold is pronounced 3280 half guilders, in pieces of 10 and 5 guilders.

Thus, the coin base, now introduced in Austria, was created for the gold money.

Now, however, it was decided to change the name of the unit of value; it should be counted on crowns; The definition of the crown, of course historically, is: a crown means half a florin of Austrian currency.

The future gold pieces, at 20 and 10 crowns, should therefore be so beaten that out of the kilogram of fine gold come 3280 crowns in those gold pieces. But this is not the definition of the crown, as we know.

This results in the Münzpari against Germany:
1 gulden in the new gold money = 1.70 marks (so not about 2 Mark, which would have corresponded to the coin pari of 1857);
or 1 crown = 0.85 marks.

Furthermore, the idea hovered in the spirit of the legislator that the valutary position was to be procured for this new cash payment: it was not said, for this concept was lacking; it was not done for the time being, for reasons that we will have to consider later; but it was floating, because other ways of the exodromic attachment were not in prospect at that time. -

Supposing that the new cash had already become valutary, it was to be expected that smaller and short-lasting fluctuations in the exchange rate against the gold countries would be compensated for in the often described automatic manner, by sending or receiving the valuta cash. These machines were considered sufficient: the question whether it was this for large and long-lasting deviations from the agreed parity has not yet been raised. -

In order to put this into practice, a large stock of gold was needed, for this metal, which had now become hylic, was necessary for the technical production of the new cash; it had to come to expression, as it is said; But it did not have to be pronounced - which meant that at first only commercial coins were produced, but it was also to be proclaimed, which is taken for granted and is therefore not mentioned.

This gold reserve could have been bought; it would only have come down to offering prices that would have seemed advantageous to the owner of gold - be it coins or bars - then he likes to part with the precious material. But what does buy mean? The Austrian state could have offered the price only in its valutary money (ie in notes); But the owner would have had to determine the price in these notes, since, as we know, it is impossible for any state to purchase gold - or any other commodity - at fixed prices, not even from other countries in which chrysodromia prevails this device works only for the owner of other money of the chrysodromic state.

From this it follows that large purchases of gold had to depress the Austrian Intervalutary rate against the neighboring gold countries incalculably, while one wanted to receive the course at that time height.

For these reasons, a completely different way had to be chosen for gold procurement (better: acquisition): the so-called bond. Austria had the necessary amount of gold delivered, and promised, after the amount had been converted into future cash, to regard the suppliers of that amount as a creditor and to pay that debt so and so high, with interest being paid in future cash to pay. Only because of the restored equilibrium in the national budgets was this promise accepted. So Austria did not buy that reserve of gold, but exchanged it for very strong pension obligations, which were payable in future cash. So the public debt was increased accordingly; that they were at the same time somewhat diminished by the conversion of other older government bonds is correct, but is not considered here. The acquisition of gold thus brought about an increase in state costs, ie greater taxpayer benefits.

The consideration of how high the annual pension was to be determined lay with those who wanted to supply the metal; this is of course expected; but the amount of the pension can not be calculated: it is based on a decision of the opponents, since, as one easily forgets, there is no equation which states that given money has a fixed relation to promised pensions. These two sizes do not allow for a necessary relationship. The capital that I give in money at once, and the money I spend on it, have no inner relation to each other, since present money and future money are completely incomparable, even if the monetary system continues unchanged. Capital and rent are as incomparable as rye and wheat, as are cattle and sheep, as long as it is observation; if they are to be compared - and they should - it can only be done by decision, which is ultimately based on balancing of power. So here, too, the power of the people who gave the gold was decisive; the state, which was bound to have this metal, was forced to accept the conditions of rent. The fact is that the acquisition of the gold was successful, and that the mints of Austria carried out the transformation into coins, the state, however, carried out the proclamation. -

How much gold, this metal *al marco* considers, has now acquired the monarchy?

In doing so, we ignore the consequences of the new constitution of 1867, which created a cis and trans-leithanic half with special financial administration. Both laws are consistent in content, although they are well distinguished under state law. The distribution of the burden was such that 70,000 fell to the countries represented in the Reich Parliament, 30,000 to the Kingdom of Hungary. The Law on Gold Loans for the countries represented in the Reich Parliament is dated August 2, 1892, and therefore covers only 70,000 of the total gold purchase, while the remainder of 30,000 was to be acquired by the Kingdom of Hungary in a similar manner.

If we now summarize what happens to the entire Austro-Hungarian monarchy, the result is as follows: the tax administrations were authorized to purchase so much gold *al marco* by way of loan, so that the amount of 312 million guilders would be obtained by converting currency into gold coins of the Crown currency, according to the above mentioned coinage. So far went the authorization that in new pieces of gold the amount of 624 million crowns could be produced (twice as much as the above-mentioned amount in gulden of Austrian currency); 70% of this amount to 436.8 million crowns for the countries represented in the Reich Parliament; 30% are 187.2 million crowns for the Kingdom of Hungary.

However, this authorization did not make full use of it, but the inordinately large purchases of gold (in bars or gold coins treated in cash) initially had the effect of restoring the monarchy's reputation for financial standing.

With the expression of this mass in gold pieces of 20 and 10 crowns was begun immediately; and this technical business continued its quiet progress. The new gold pieces were not placed on the market, but carefully locked up and monitored until it was otherwise by law. But why was this amount of gold purchased?

The state did not say so, but every connoisseur, for example from Inama-Sternegg, could guess (Zeitschrift für Volkswirtschaft, Vienna 1892, Volume I, p. 644):
The amount of government notes that belonged to the entire monarchy was 312 million guilders of Austrian currency; Obviously, it was the acquisition of gold that was intended to "cover" precisely these states, or more precisely: cover gold with the new hylic metal. This means that those notes should first be turned into chrysogenous, but provisionally still necessary money.

The deeper meaning, according to the theory at the time, was, however, that those notes of state were to be redeemed in a later time, to be given by future laws, in the new cash gold. All that was needed then was to put aside the paper notes that had been collected at the coffers, put them out of the way and burn them as waste, and that bad money, which came from the misfortune of 1866, disappeared.

It was taken for granted that then the state would treat the new gold money valutarily; as well as that the state would again enable the Austro-Hungarian Bank - for this title had been adopted by the former National

Bank since 1878 - to redeem its notes. Thus a gold standard would have arisen, quite according to the silver currency, which from 30 August 1858 to 27 April 1859 had really existed. Fluctuations in the rate of exchange between the neighboring gold countries would then, it was thought, be automatically regulated. Of the banknotes, which were to become redeemable, no disturbance was to be feared.

There is no doubt that this plan was foreseen: the valutary money was to be cashed with the hylic metals gold; the banknotes should continue to exist as accessory money with redeemability.

But what should happen to the silver gulden of the Austrian currency? Partly they could be converted into silver mint coins; but what remained of that, one did not yet know exactly what to do with it, and left it in thoughts still undecided.

This plan corresponded entirely to what the metallistic theorists had prepared as advice: bar constitution of valutary money. The abandonment of the hylic metals silver and the transition to the hylic metals gold was supported by the metallists for the most whimsical reasons, as if it were due to changed properties of these metals, while it was due to the changed position of these metals in the neighboring countries; but that does not matter here; In any case, the advice of those metallists coincided with what was necessary to prepare an automatic settlement of the inter-valutary rates against the countries of the gold standard. Furthermore, every strict monometallist had to demand that the silver gulden of Austrian currency be removed from the new monetary system, just as it had been demanded in the German Reich by these confessors that the thalers should be disposed of after 1871. -

But soon after 1892 a great disappointment occurred.
The inter-valutary rate against the gold countries did not adjust to the newly created exchange rate, but rather unfavorable for Austria. The guilder (that is, 2 kroner) did not show the exchange rate of 1.70 mark on the stock exchange as expected, but stood lower. Judged by that coin pari, the German currency therefore had a premium, and the Austrian

valutary money a disagreement - despite the almost complete coverage of the national notes.

The greatest horror occurred on 9 and 10 November 1893; At that time, on the Vienna Stock Exchange, 100 marks did not cost about 117.56 kroner, as it corresponds to the exchange par, but 125.50 kroner; the premium was 6.75%! (See tables on monetary statistics, third edition, 5th issue, Vienna 1905, page 516.)

But nothing is more natural than that; because the inter-valutary course arises pantopolisch and can be held only by exodromic devices, automatic or other, on a certain height, for example on the coin paris. But where were these facilities? They were still missing completely.

The fact that the notes of the states were fully covered by the new gold money, and that the banknotes also returned to adequate cover, means nothing at all for the exchange-rate course; only the metallists think it because they take all those notes as a promise to pay, but not as an independent means of payment with nominal value. But even if one thinks of promises to pay, so it does not matter whether the debtor can pay, but whether he really pays - and he did not. For the Austrian state has created the new gold money technically and provided it with proclamatory validity - but he did not raise it in the year 1892 and also later in valutary position. Therefore, this innovation could do nothing to keep the intervalutary course on the exchange. Unfavorable economic conditions could and did occur, so that the disagreement between the Austrian valuta money (that is, the two types of paper notes) against Germany is quite understandable.

If the state had begun to issue the new gold money drop by drop, it would have been advantageous to sell it to the neighboring gold countries; the already existing incarceration was thus anxiously maintained for this new reason.

Many people who are unaware of the nature of the intervalutary course fell into a sad mood over the new facility, which failed only because it was piecemeal. Because the thought: "Bar constitution in gold for valutary money" was not executed; the bare money was created, but valutary it was not. -

In the meantime, however, the state itself, which we recognize from the actions of senior men, has lost its element in the idea of reform. Just as the leading German statesman, Bismarck, had enforced the retention of the coins by a word of force, and thereby created the emergency currency with us, the Austrian statesmen have developed strong reservations as to whether it is really necessary to raise all the necessary money with the new gold money replace.

The obvious example of the German Reich was encouraging; If, in Germany, the taler which had become more expensive was retained in addition to the new gold money of 1871, as a currant money (although in an accessory position since 1876), why should one not do the same in Austria with the silver gulden?

The silver gulden was thus, as a necessary money with silver plate, quietly left in the capacity as a currant money; at the low price of the London silver price he had a negative metallopolic agio, which excited all metallists; but in other circles one did not think long about this case, because the silver gulden had also been previously currency; his newly created notality (since 1879) is an invisible property that remained all the more hidden as the silver plate is undoubtedly a piece of precious metal.

The common man knows nothing about hylic or non-hylic metals. So it was extremely easy to pass the silver gulden over to the new money system as a notional, subordinate moneylender. The state, which had no interest in holding back this substandard type of money in its coffers, even occasionally paid with this variety, although in principle it offered only banknotes and government notes. And this gave the impression to the people as if the state were willing to make occasional cash payments - for by 1879 the silver gulden had been cash money; the notation had not been understood; There was not even a word for this process, for the phrase "demonetization of silver" that appeared here and there was as clumsy as possible, since silver coins had not ceased to hold. -

There was also the question of whether the state would really redeem the paper notes of the state, 312 million guilders of Austrian currency, in golden crowns. The layman wanted to recognize in his metallistic attitude whether the reform was being taken seriously or not: he was anxious to see the paper notes disappear.

The leading statesmen have now thought: the paper notes should disappear on our account, otherwise the people think that everything is unsuccessful; but it can be replaced by other necessary money, especially by silver coins. Then his will was done to the people; Prejudices must be spared.

Only one reservation remained: how will the inter-valutary rate be set against the gold countries? One can imagine that the statesmen politely requested the advice of the Austro-Hungarian bank management; and it would not be conspicuous if the well-informed leaders had replied to the bank: "We'll get it."

Such events can not be documented, but from the later course of the reform it is certain that something similar must have happened.
And so we come to the last act of reform.

The preparatory laws of 2 August 1892 were followed by an imperial decree of 21 September 1899 (parliamentary difficulties were to blame for first choosing the form of a decree). In it a meaningful plan for the elimination of the paper government notes was set up and also carried out within a short time.

In order to understand this somewhat complicated operation, it is especially important to keep this in mind: those states' notes have not been replaced in traffic by the corresponding amount of new gold coins. If we think of the business as having been carried out in its entirety, for which a certain period of time was required, the result is not that the corresponding amount of gold coins would then have been on the market instead of those paper-based government notes.

Instead, those paper notes have been replaced by other notional types of money, namely:

1. partly by silver coins, of which, as we shall see, there are two kinds;

2. partly by silver currency coins, namely gulden pieces of the Austrian currency; Since 1879 the coinage of silver guilder pieces is no longer free, these silver gulden pieces no longer belong to the cash, but to the emergency. The fact that these gulden pieces are still counted as cash in Austria is based on the idea that currant money made of precious metals should always be regarded as cash money, and therefore based on another concept of cash. But everything is darkened! According to our definition such a confusion is not possible at all: what distinguishes the silver gulden from the golden crown money (not technically) is the fact that the silver gulden have become deserted, while now only the golden crown money has the bare property.

3. Finally, some of the paper notes have been replaced by notes of the Austro-Hungarian Bank, the notability of which is clear.

Other types of replacement have not taken place, so the paper notes have been completely replaced by other notional money, some of which have silver plates, some papers; **But the paper money types are now banknotes, not notes of the state.**

This is the result of the conversion of those paper notes in the amount of 312 million guilders.

To this end, the state has spent: First, as much silver as was necessary to produce small coins in the amount of $40 + 32 = 72$ million guilders of Austrian currency. This silver did not have to be bought first; one could win it from the Hungarian mines, or one could turn stocks of silver gulden, which were in state coffers, into those minor coins with a very large coinage; for the silver gulden has a far higher specific content than that given to the new coins.

Second, the total state spent: 160 + 80 = 240 million gulden of Austrian currency in the new golden kroner. This amount in new gold coins was handed over to the Austro-Hungarian Bank, which took over the duty to redeem state notes: partly in silver gulden; partly in banknotes denominated in guilders and consisting of pieces of 10, 100 and 1000 guilders; partly in banknotes, which represented a new type in which they were 10 crowns.

State notes, which were cashed at public coffers, destroyed the state; those who redeemed the bank had the bank destroyed by the state.

The silver gulden that came into circulation are not redeemable in golden crown money; the banknotes of the older and the newer types, which have been marketed by that operation, are not redeemable in golden crown money, at least for the time being, even if there is a political intention to bring about later redemption of banknotes.

According to this, the paper government notes, in the amount of 312 million guilders of Austrian currency, are replaced by nothing more than money; As far as these kinds of money possess silver plates, they have a disagio (in the sense of the internal Agios, see P. 153), which is to be calculated according to the respective Londoner silver prices; the banknotes have such a discount of 100 per cent of their validity; but here we mean only the loss that would be suffered by the use of the money in a plateau, which, of course, nobody thinks of. The validity of all these types of money, like all types of money in general, is proclamatory and is not affected by that disagreement. There is no talk of intervalutarian agio here.

The stocks of gold coins, which the state had acquired by way of that gold loan at 4% interest rates, were not quite as large as was appropriate to the given authorization, since not all bonds had been issued. From the actual advance, 240 million guilders of Austrian currency were given to the bank, which is thus fully prepared for future redemption of its notes.

The remainder of the gold remains in the hands of the two state governments.

Specifically, it is still to catch up on the redemption of the state notes: -

40 million guilders were redeemed by the state in silver coins with the validity of 1 crown.
From the kilogram of coin silver of the fineness 835/1,000 200 pieces are beaten. Such coins must be accepted in traffic up to a value of 50 crowns.

32 million guilders were redeemed in silver coins with the value of 5 kroner; such must be accepted in traffic up to the amount of 250 crowns. From the kilogram of coin silver of the fineness 900/1,000 41 2/3 pieces are beaten.

The Bank must redeem 160 million guilders, either in silver gulden (which is the bullion currency) or in older notes of the bank, to 10 florins and more, which are also due to the general assumption of compulsion according to our terminology as currency, but with paper plates.

The Bank must redeem 80 million guilders in newly created banknotes of 10 kroner, which are fully covered and must remain.

This gives information about the state notes in the amount of 312 million guilders.

Furthermore, the money types of the Austrian currency are abolished: the thalers and the minor coins; on the other hand, those are preserved: the silver gulden pieces and the gulden banknotes.

New for the crown currency were: the gold pieces; silver coins of 5 crowns and 1 crown; the very small coins made of base metal; and the banknotes to 10 kroner.

The newly created gold money, which partly rests in the bank, partly in the state coffers, is not treated as valuta. neither the public coffers nor the bank are in principle prepared to use this money for payments; only now and then do they keep it ready, but in principle they pay in banknotes or in the silver gulden that has become urgent.

From this it follows that the valutary money of the monarchy is even further from the year 1900 onwards; There is money (the new gold coins), but it has an accessory position, and still has the peculiar quality that on purpose it is only occasionally put into circulation.

This cash, because it is accessory, could very easily receive an agio; because it is due to the chrysoleptic constitution of the western neighboring countries easily convertible into German, French or English cash money. Those neighboring states represent thus a market area, which offers a fixed price in the neighbor money for Austrian gold coins. But the delivery of Austrian gold coins has, from a business point of view, a meaning only if the exchange rate (for which only value-added money comes into consideration) moves away from the new exchange pari, in the unfavorable direction for Austria.

However, as already explained, this inter-valutary price is kept at the level of the exhange pari by a very special exodromic activity of the bank. As long as this happens, no agio of Austrian gold coins is to be feared for reasons of gold trading. -

In order to understand psychologically the behavior of the State as a whole with regard to the silver coins, it must be remembered that not only are metallic views generally prevalent, but that they prevail in the bimetallic manner established by the French legislation of 1803. At that time a hylische position had really been given to both metals, the gold and the silver. So there was the silver currency, as well as the golden really cash money - but only until 1876. From then on, the silver money remained currency (namely the pieces at 5 Fr.), but the trusteeship was no longer available after 1876.

But the laymen did not understand this, for they had become accustomed to consider all currency with plates of precious metal as cash, that is, the silver pieces at 5 Fr.; The redeeming of notes in the pieces that became notional at 5 Fr. was regarded as a redemption in France, even after 1876, because the French did not know the correct concept of cash.

The Austrian state, as well as the public, were also dominated by this idea, which is quite amateur, and the strange situation occurred that the Austrian state, if it took on this prejudice, the greatest part of the public opinion on its while the same prejudice afforded financial relief, it was not necessary to sell the many gold money that had been procured, but to keep it in the coffers, after satisfying the bank's claims.
Any enthusiast for bar constitution of valutary money would have to reproach this; we do not blame it, we just point out that it happened.

In the light of all these obvious circumstances, which we have presented here without cloaking phrases of silver-saturated traffic, metal coverage, overflowing paper grades, and the like, it must now be asked whether there is a lytropolitical interest in raising Austrian cash into valutary status ? There is no such interest; for other than lytropolitischen reasons one can do it yes.

The contrary opinion, as prevalent as it is, believes that an exodromic regulation of the inter-valutary rates against the neighboring gold countries must always be achieved in that automatic manner; then, however, the cash money of Austria would have to be raised in valutary position.

But the main thing is that there is some kind of exodromic administration, and that is the case in Austria, since the bank has taken on this task and successfully solves it. This follows from the following overview.

For 100 Mk., The average price paid on the Vienna Stock Exchange was:
1893: 121.33 crowns
1894: 122.22 "

1895: 119,20 "

So still more, than the exchange rate (117.56 crowns) equivalent.

But after the regulation had come, we find:
1896: 117.72 crowns
1897: 117.47 "
1898: 117.69 "
1899: 117.93 "
1900: 118.21 "
1901: 117.36 "
1902: 117.15 "
1903: 117.19 "
1904: 117.32 "
so very insignificant, sometimes no agio. (See tables on currency statistics, third edition, 5th issue, Vienna 1905, p. 516.)

Thus, it is no longer necessary to give the cash money the still lacking value valutary position, that is, among other things, the cash in cash (ie in gold pieces) redeem.

On the other hand, the objections raised are based on the anticipated "real" satisfaction, which, since we also regard the state as a payment community in Austria, is of no importance whatsoever. -

Thus the Austrian state, which has been haunted by unheard-of political examinations, has produced the present monetary constitution, which offers fixed inter-valutary rates, without the valued property being lent to the cash. It does not need to surprise us, however, that this course fortification does not come in vain, for it only occurs everywhere where the necessary sacrifices can be made. In this way Austria has widened the sphere of experience, albeit very much against his will, so that it is now easy to create the missing theory for the financial system: **the state perceives itself as a payment community and does not pay attention to foreign people. He creates for his legal life the concept of the unit of value, which he defines historically; the means of payment receive proclamation by the state; Some, but not all means of payment have also metal content, which is just because the validity does not**

depend on the content, so tolerate this or that content. From this foundation, the action of the state becomes comprehensible, whether we observe it in the case of a bar constitution or in the event of a provisional constitution of the value money.

But the completeness of the Lytrian administration still includes the exodromy, which is practically recognized only in modern times. Since we have presented all this from the point of view of the state, and not according to private wishes or advice, it is justifiable to call the theory presented, though it actually embraces all means of payment, the most important example as the state theory of money.

The metallists deserve all recognition as practitioners; they want a cash constitution of valutary money, so they have a very simple, generally understandable goal: why should not they recommend it for reasons that are understandable to the public? That goal is included in the theory of the state as a special case, so, from that point on, it encounters no objection.

But state theory has also to accommodate the many other forms of payment and to uncover their common root; therefore it must be more comprehensive and tolerant than the theory of metal, from which we bid farewell without hope, and hopefully forever. (Here ends the "State Theory of Money" in the first edition [1905]: supplements and additions.

§ 19 c. The customs payment in Austria 1854 to 1900

The monetary system in Austria is even more complicated than it appears in the above description; There is a very important area of business where there are special rules for payment: customs business. They form "exceptions," as they say. But the more correct view is that customs have a special monetary structure. So the state does not have a single monetary system, but has two adjacent to each other, whose application is separated according to business. The customs payments are under special law, in contrast to the other payments, which are under the "common" rights. Only the system for "base" payments is discussed above. Both systems run side by side without being disturbed: thus one has an example of the so-called parallel currency, which is not uncommon otherwise.

The special right for customs payments did not come into being until 1854, for the following reason. In 1854 the Austrian monarchy was in a state of great power; but in financial terms Austria was weak at the time. Only through a big loan could the funds be found to set up armies because of the Crimean War and to put the bank back in a position to accept their cash payments. But the bond could only be successful, especially in neighboring Germany, if the interest were not paid "in paper", not according to the common law valid since 1848, but in "sounding" coin. This explains the three arrangements of the patent of 26 June 1854 - which is to remember that the former bank notes were denominated in guilders of the Convention on foot and were irredeemable:

"1. A loan of at least 350 million and no more than 500 million guilders shall be made by way of a subscription to be opened to the extent of the whole monarchy.

"2. The issue of the loan will take place at the price of 95 guilder bank value for every 100 guilders in government bonds.

"3. The government bonds will bear interest at this loans of 5% in silver or gold coin, the gold does not fold with higher values than the 15 ½ of silver to be adopted."

At first we want to refrain from paying in gold, which has little or no practicality, and thus note: the interest was essentially in silver; more precisely in silver coins; and usually in gulden pieces of the Convention foot; It was not until 1858 that for every 100 gulden pieces of this older type, 105 gulden pieces were given according to the law of 1857 ("Austrian currency").

No doubt, therefore: for the redemption of the coupons cash payment takes place, while otherwise the treasury paid in 1854 in the valutary banknotes; so special right.

Does the state pay in this case in cash - as it were out of love of order? No. He pays cash because he then pays in a metal that formed the basis of the currency in the other states of the German Confederation. Namely, the state pays these interest rates in a kind of coin which was easily convertible into the money of the German neighboring states (for the silver was unlimited in Germany).

But where should the Austrian tax authorities take many silver coins at the two annual interest payments? His taxes go into banknotes; the silver mines are unlikely to yield enough yield; So you would have had to buy silver coins with banknotes.

But one did not do that, but treated some revenue of the state differently than before. Until then, the tariffs had been paid in accordance with common law, ie in the main areas of the empire in banknotes (only in the Lombardy-Venetian kingdoms it was different). So it had been until the year 1854, for, as we are told by Herr I. von Gruber from the k. k. refer to the Ministry of Finance in Vienna, can be found on customs payments no special provision, either in the political Law Collection (1790-1848) still in Reichsgesetzblatt (Law Gazette), which has been published since 1849. Until then, the customs payment in the countries where the paper was forced to go through was part of the payments that could be made in paper. It is learned on this occasion that the customs duties in the crown lands with paper circulation at that time, 1854, amounted to about 12 million guilders annually.

Then the state decided: from now on customs duties will be "levied in silver" (order of the Ministry of Finance of July 5, 1854), first in pieces of the Convention.
The principle: tariffs are raised in silver, from then until 1878 existed with a brief but very instructive interruption.

This provided a source for the purchase of silver: the payer of the Customs must see to it that he presents silver coins; If this payer lives in

Germany, he may (Order of July 9, 1854) probably also apply German silver coins; If the payer lives in Austria, as is usually the case, he must buy the necessary silver coins. As a result, the silver agio tends to rise, but the burden is not borne by the treasury, as it would have been if the treasury purchased the silver coins. **The treasury thus pushes the payment of the premium to the customs payer; if they want to defend themselves, they can not do it; because the state declares: the customs payment is under special law.**

In this way certain payments to the State and certain other payments by the State to its interest creditors were linked to a system of payment in monetary terms, and the purpose is: the Treasury should be redeemed from the dangers of the paper economy, not through cessation of paper payment at all, but by their non-application to those two businesses, one of which means spending for the state, the other revenue.

Of course, **the tax authorities have two things to do from there on: revenue and expenditure in the form of a monetary coin; furthermore income and expenditure in paper**. Each of the two bills takes place in a different unit of value: there it is called "gulden in silver", here it is called "gulden" par excellence, which is - practically - in paper. How much the "gulden in silver" is worth in paper depends on stock market prices.

Note that unity has been lost: there are now two independent value units side by side.

With the payment in sounding coin the paper money is excluded in principle. On the other hand, when paying in gulden par excellence, the paper money is always permissible; the payment in silver coins is not inadmissible; it just is not required.

The paper "only" applies in the one, the common payment system; but the silver coin (the convention gulden piece in 1854) is valid in each of the two systems: it is both a gulden in silver and a gulden par excellence; but since the piece has agio, the payer does not use it for ordinary payments.

The two kinds of bookkeeping in the State central treasury are certainly inconvenient; but this can not be seriously considered in relation to the advantage that the state achieves: in bond issues, it is treated on the German stock exchanges as though cash payment were taking place. Of course, in other matters the uncertainty of the exchange rate remains; For the state has saved only itself, as an economic person, from the evil, but not the people living in its territory. It is not the state territory that is freed from the fluctuating exchange rates, but only the treasury, though not generally, but in relation to those transactions. -

But supposing that the fluctuating exchange rates ceased, for instance as a result of the bank going over to cash payment - then the special bill for "gulden in silver" and "gulden par excellence" would be superfluous - and that would be the reason for levying the Tariffs in silver have been dropped. This guess of the reader is correct. For it is indeed read in the Reichsgesetzblatte (Law Gazette) with a pleasant surprise that during the time of the cash payment of 1858-59 the collection of tariffs in silver did not take place. It was also possible to pay customs duties in banknotes in those months. But as soon as the warlike prospects in 1859, the cash payment, hardly begun, was again set up again, the levying of tariffs in silver came out again immediately. This is the meaning of the decree of the Ministry of Finance of April 29, 1859, which states:

"By this, the decrees of September 23 and December 30, 1858.... , by which the acceptance of banknotes denominated in Austrian currency or on convention coins was permitted for the payment of these fees was rendered inoperative for the whole Reich. "

In other words, customs payment in silver was unnecessary during the short period of cash payment, because at that time the exchange rates against Germany were in line with exchage pari and were therefore fixed; as soon as they began to waver again and became unfavorable to Austria, the customs levy in silver recommenced, because the Treasury once again needed the safeguard for the lodging of its bonds. Strange remains the cold-bloodedness, with which the state burdens the victims, which arise from the agio, the customs payers. The higher the premium, the more the tariff payer must make an effort to acquire the necessary silver; the more difficult it is, in particular, to import into Austria. It strengthened the trade policy effect of the Agio: while the growing agio already brings a certain easing of the export, at the same time importation is made more difficult because of the silver tariffs. But this is desirable in mercantilist states, and so one may even like to have seen this side effect. -

So far we have assumed that the duties were payable in silver gulden pieces, ie in 1854 in the old, from 1858 on in the new pieces. But there were also gold coins allowed, both domestic and foreign. The decree of the Ministry of Finance of July 9, 1854 states:
"Customs payments also include Austrian ducats. their value (that is, their validity) is 4 gulden 33 3/4 cruiser of the twenty gulden foot; also the golden Twenty Franc piece is accepted; its value (that is, its validity) is: 7 guilders 42 kreuzer of the twenty gulden foot; etc. ".
This assumption was withdrawn from foreign gold coins by the decree of the Ministry of Finance of 4 November 1856.

However, the fact remains that temporary payment of tariffs in silver could also be effected by transferring - gold coins; not according to their fluctuating value on the stock market, but according to firm, proclamatory sentences.

It is clear from this: the "gulden in silver", which governs customs payments, is not a coin; but is the value unit for customs payment. The piece of silver was considered such a "guilder in silver"; and the golden dukat in this shop was 4 gulden 33 3/4 cruisers (60 of which go to the gulden).

The establishment of tariffs "in silver" lost all meaning when the agony of the silver gulden disappeared in the summer of 1878. This event, which is presumed to be known here (see above), is known to be a true revelation - about the nature of money and will remain unforgotten as such. Here, however, one can only ask: if the silver gulden no longer has an agio against the valutary notes, as it really has been since June 1878 -

what is the point of raising the tariffs in silver? Answer: none. For the holders of maturing coupons of the silver-bearing bonds no longer have the slightest interest in redemption in silver; they also like to take notes, because they do not want the metal in silver, but the metal that can be transformed into German money.

But if the holders of the coupons, despite their right, no longer insist on the silver payment, why should the state still impose tariffs in silver? Nothing is more comprehensible than that he soon neglected to do so. From 1878, the customs levy in silver has really stopped. The epoch, which began in 1854, was over after about 24 years. As a side effect of the disappearance of the silver agio we recognize the way of the silver payment at customs.

At the same time, however, the Treasury had an unexpected effect. He had meant: since I am paying in silver, the German market is open to me for loans.

But since 1871, the silver in the German Reich had taken the property of unlimited expression and Germany had administratively entered into the gold standard since 1876. From then on, the German owner of those Austrian coupons was less and less satisfied that their redemption took place in silver, for silver was no longer physically convertible into German money. Of course, the German pensioner wanted to know what he received for the preserved silver gulden at the banker in Mark; However, when he received no more in German money than for the gulden paper, Austria's silver pensions lost all preference over the paper pensions. As a result, the Treasury fell back into the situation that it had wanted to avoid by paying silver; the silver clause remained legal, but its economic effect disappeared, for the silver pensions, like the paper pensions, made all fluctuations in the exchange rate.

But if Austria still wants bonds bearing fixed interest rates for the German owner, then a new type must be created. One should expect: bonds, bearish in Mark; but once again, it was better to call the metal than the foreign unit of value, and created bonds that yielded interest in gold. This has been done entirely for the same reasons as the interest in silver used to be. Because not the metal is actually meant, but the currency of the neighboring state. And in order to raise the necessary gold, the customs payer was again tense. Immediately the decree appeared that customs duties were to be paid in gold from now on (1878).

Actually, nothing has changed, if you refer all this to the currency of the neighboring country: only the name of the metal is another; but it is always the metal that has the excellent position in the currency of the neighboring country. -

The customs payment in gold still needs an explanation because of an occurring unit of value, called gulden in gold; and perhaps it is best that we say that the gold guilder is not at first what everyone should expect: it is not so much gold as was obtained after the course of 1878 for a common guilder. The gulden in gold is therefore not found from the gold prices as it presented back then, 1878.

Furthermore, the gold gulden still has a peculiarity.
In Austria in 1878 by no means there is the gold standard; yes, in the then existing monetary system, there was no gold piece. I do not say that there were no Austrian gold pieces; for example, there were ducats and another piece of gold, but these golden pieces lacked the proclamation of gulden par excellence. So these coins were outside the "common" monetary system. Such pieces are called trade coins.

Now, if the payment of the customs duty was to take place in gold, that was not a payment in the existing cash of the common payment system; In 1878 this system had silver money as a cash (admittedly only until January 1879), but gold money did not have it, and therefore not as cash.

There is a big difference in this: from 1854 on, when the tariffs were paid in silver, the silver money used for this - as far as domestic coins were used - was at the same time cash of the common payment system.

In the transition to the payment of tariffs in gold but this fact could not be imitated. One had to make golden trade coins of Austrian character for customs money, for example ducats or the other trade coin minted since 1870, the eight- and four-gulden piece, which has so far remained unmentioned.

The creation of the eight- and four-gulden piece by the law of March 9, 1870 is very remarkable. Apparently at that time the transition to the gold currency or perhaps bimetallism was to be prepared in the sense of the French law of 1803, while the "Austrian currency" of existed in 1857 with their training. In the same way one did not immediately change the monetary constitution, but created only a new type of coins, namely a piece of gold, which was technically exactly the French 20 Franc (or ten-potions) imitated. The larger of these pieces was given the inscription: "8 fl. - 20 Fr."; the smaller one: "4 fl.-10 Fr.". This is just as understandable for the Mint technic as it is strange for the connoisseur of the monetary system. For how does the Austrian state get to give this coin the inscription 20 Frank or 10 Frank? Does she mean so much? In Austria, there is no unit of value, called Frank; because you expect gulden.

And whether in countries with franc bill (France, Belgium) that piece is 20 francs, that has to be decided by France and Belgium, but not by Austria. The coinage just understands Frank under the gold piece a certain content, and that alone should be said in the inscription.

But further: what does the inscription 8 Fl. ? About that you could pay eight gulden of Austrian currency? Not at all. You could not pay anything with this coin; it lacked the proclamatory validity of value units, despite the inscription. The inscription does not decide on the validity; the law has to talk and - it was silent. Accordingly, the inscription "8 fl." Only means that Austrian coin technicians will now understand by gulden - with the addition "in gold" - a certain value, not actual, but legal content, namely the eighth part of the value had that Austrian 20 Frank piece.

It is very probable that Austria was considering releasing the stamp of the eight and four-piece coin (as in France in 1803) and declaring that common payments of 8 gulden of Austrian currency can also be made with this piece; then you would have had bimetallism. Maybe you also wanted to omit the silver expression then; that would have led to the gold standard in the French way. But neither one nor the other has happened. Those golden eight- and four-piece pieces remained outside the money for base payments and eventually, for a time, found a modest living in the system of tariff money.

The form of these coins is shown in the tables for monetary statistics, written in k. k. Ministry of Finance, Vienna 1893, Table 26 (page 49) for each of the calendar years 1870 to 1892 information. It follows that for all these years they have been co-written:

a) eight-gulden pieces. , , , , , 8 448 399 pieces
b) four-gulden pieces. , , , , , , , 889 039   "
in amount:
a) 67 587 192 gold guilders
b) 3 556 156 gold guilders
together: 71 143 348 gold guilders.

Since the expression began in 1870 and ceased in 1892, this statement is exhaustive.
After this explanation, the Austrian customs payment will be easy to describe.

When it was declared on December 27, 1878: from now on the duties are raised in gold, it was added: the golden eight-gulden piece is usable for the payment of 8 fl. Customs debt. But that means: there is now a third unit of value in Austria, namely: first, the gulden par excellence; secondly, the guilder in silver, which was still used because of the interest payments on the previously discussed bonds, but no longer in the customs; and finally, third, the gold guilder, often called gold guilders. All three value units are independent of each other: their mutual interchangeability is determined on the stock exchange, as a result of the demand and the offer; with the one casual coincidence that the florin in silver, since 1878 in June, no longer has a premium, for the silver gulden piece is no longer to be used with advantage as a plate, while at the same time it is also proclaimed gulden par excellence. By contrast, the eight-gulden piece is only suitable for customs payments; it has no proclamatory validity in "gulden par excellence".

The political reason for the change requires no new explanation: the state, which wants to interest certain bonds in gold, raised its tariffs in gold, in order to obtain for that interest a part of the means of payment. Just as it had been with the silver.

In addition to the native eight- and four-gulden pieces but foreign gold coins were declared acceptable, and mainly: foreign 20 Franc piece, which were technically equal to the Austrian 8 Gulden piece; and also German gold pieces of 20 and 10 Mk.

These pieces, however, had to be validated for the new unit of value in "gold guilders" in order to be usable. It was based on the proper salary (the foreign 20 Franc piece therefore had 8 gold gulden in customs transactions, the twenty-twenty-mark coin had 9.88 gold gulden in the customs business), and it was strictly insisted that no worn-out items flowed into the coffers. The result was the following peculiarity: French and German gold coins were not common money in Austria, but they were customs money there; a strange Synchartism: first, because not mutually, but one-sidedly, because that the Austrian eight-gulden piece in itself in France and its allied states would have accepted acceptance, that could be no question.

Second, but strange, because the foreign pieces were only money for customs payments; that is, a one-sided and at the same time limited to certain business synarchism.

Another relief was allowed to the customs payers. If they did not have any of the approved gold coins, they could also apply Austrian (not foreign) silver coins; but that was not a payment of the tariff in silver gulden, but it was something completely different: instead of the gold coins actually required, they were allowed to pay their price in silver coins, according to the average state in the last month. The difference is clear; the silver coins are not valid for gold gulden, so they are not valid in customs payments; but they have validity only with common payment. But the customs administration, instead of the actual means of payment, also accepted its price, as it were ready to purchase the gold coins for themselves.

It was quite impossible to pay the price of the gold pieces about in banknotes, because the state wanted that the customers themselves brought the golden means of payment - or at least the price in silver, at least the means to the payments of the state in gold and those in silver gathered.

Consider that on the day of this decree (December 27, 1878) there was still no certainty as to whether the Agio for silver, which had disappeared in June, 1878, would be permanently absent. But as it did not happen, the strict rule, "or the price in silver coins," had no purpose. Nonetheless, the rule was maintained, with the idea that a silver guilder would be even better than a paper guilder if he did not have a premium.

When, in 1892, the new laws were prepared, which prepared the crown currency, new gold coins were foreseen therein: the pieces of twenty and ten crowns. At the same time, in the same law, the coinage of the eight and four-piece pieces was discontinued. Thus, this coin disappears, practically considered, almost entirely. But what does not disappear is the value unit "gold guilders". Customs duties were still levied on gold florins, and the twenty- and ten-crown coins were used as a means of payment for customs duties by recognizing, for each 100 crowns in the new gold pieces, 42 gold florins.

From this emerges the peculiar case, which the tariff-payers probably never quite understood and whose systematic accommodation is most instructive:
I have 100 crowns in the new (1892 created) gold money in hand. Now

I have two kinds of business: First, I want to pay taxes; then those 100 crowns are no more and not less than 50 guilders. Second, I do not want to pay taxes but customs; then those 100 crowns are only 42 guilders.

But nothing is easier to understand:
There is an Austrian unit of value, called gulden (par excellence); Thereafter, the taxes are measured. 100 crowns are known in this system, 50 guilders (par excellence); there is also an Austrian unit of value for customs payments, called gold gulden; 100 crowns are 42 guilders in this system.

And if there were still seven other units of value, each for special business, then seven more such registrations of the same piece of gold would be possible for twenty crowns. The same piece can be valid in different systems! -

This phenomenon, which has hitherto received little attention, must be called inner syncharchism.

Just as the Vereins-taler, the piece of silver created in 1857, had 3 marks in Germany since 1871 and 1 1/2 guilders in Austria, so that there were two different payment systems, so it is here too: the new piece of gold has two purposes.

The other coins of the crown currency, for example the numerous pieces of silver (remember the silver gulden, the five-crowned piece, the one-crowned piece) are proclaimed only for common payments; the use in the customs payment system is excluded. Exactly the same as for the silver coins, applies to the banknotes.

It has always been demanded in the case of customs payments that the coins are not over-worn; one demanded a minimum weight, be it the individual pieces, or the entire item. The reason is clear: they wanted to acquire the metal that was hylic abroad.
However, it is not a pensatory payment, as the minimum weight was a condition of acceptance, but its validity was not determined by the actual

weight. Legally, this is a difference, but in practice he does not mean much. It should be remembered, however, that the customs payment was also chart-based, but with the condition of the minimum weight maintained. Because bars were never allowed, always only coins whose validity, even if they were foreign, was always proclamatory, never was determined by weighing. -

The customs tariffs in gold guilders remained in use until 1906. Only the Customs Tariff Act of February 13, 1906, brings, one may say, a long-awaited innovation: the tariffs are set in crowns (no longer in gold guilders); for example, to quote the first line of the tariff:
Cocoa beans pay per 100 kilograms: 58 krones. Now one could believe that everything is very simple; the crown currency, introduced everywhere long ago, also applies to the customs business. That is not so. Article XVII of the above mentioned law states: "The customs duties indicated in the customs tariff, including the customs duties and the wagging fee, shall be paid in gold coin." Here gold coin means the twenty and ten crown pieces. The same article further states that foreign gold coins should also be accepted: their value (that is to say, their validity) in crown currency is fixed by ordinance.

Are customs duties, which are out of all doubt, according to crowns, payable with the money introduced since 1892? Yes or no? They are payable only in the one component of the new monetary system, namely only in the new gold coins; in the other coins and banknotes they are not.

As long as the gold coins have no agio, you notice almost nothing of this institution. But as soon as they receive an agio, the following will emerge:
No one makes any ordinary payments in the golden twenty-crown pieces; on the other hand, customs payments still have to be made in these pieces under the legal situation of 1906.

Then it becomes practically visible that there are two units of value in the domestic payment system, and that the twenty-crown piece belongs to both systems, but finds its practical use only in the payment of customs.

The state of this special bill and special payment will take so long to give up the principle that the tariffs are payable in gold coins; So as soon as the common payment for customs duties is allowed. When will that happen?
The already mentioned Article XVII of the Customs Tariff Act gives information: the two governments already agree that the special payment method of tariffs ceases as soon as the cash payments in the monarchy are resumed.

Again a most important rally, reminiscent of the short time of cash payment under the Minister Frhr. von Bruck: even then, the customs payment immediately stopped in a ringing coin.

§ 19 d. Austria-Hungary 1901 to 1914

Our account of the Austro-Hungarian monetary system ends at the end of the nineteenth century (§ 19b).
Since then, there have been some changes, which will be outlined here shortly; we bring them in four sections, increasing in importance, and begin with the changes in the coins.

I. The notes created in 1866 have been suspended since February 28, 1903, and thus no longer belong to the monetary system of the monarchy. Those are, as has been described earlier, replaced by other types of money, partly by silver coins, all of which are not redeemable or even "covered"; partly by banknotes, which also lack redeemability, but are plenty "covered" by the treasury of the bank.

The disclaimer of the state notes is only a natural consequence of the completion of the reform of 1892-1899.
The disappearance of the state notes per se, according to the then prevailing view, is considered to be more important than it seems to us, because it has by no means reached an approximation of the target "gold

currency", since the gold coins did not become valutary; but the whole system of monetary affairs has been greatly simplified. -

Likewise, it contributes to the simplification that the silver gulden (marked after the law of 1857), which were known to be included in the monetary system of 1892 as a currant money, are indeed disappearing and will soon expire the call. In fact, according to the law of March 7, 1912, they are transformed into silver coins of the crown currency - and on this occasion the new "two-crown piece" was created, which was not included in the ordinance of 1899. This new piece is an imitation of the German two-mark piece.

The coin base of the two-core piece corresponds exactly to the 1 Crown piece and also the usability as a divisional.
In detail, this process takes place in this way: Austria re-shapes: 70 million crowns in one-crown pieces; Hungary is reimagining: 30 million crowns in one-crown pieces; furthermore: Austria re-stamps: 35 million crowns in two-crown pieces; Hungary is reimagining: 15 million crowns in two-crown pieces. -

For this purpose, each of the two governments withdraws from the Austro-Hungarian bank the corresponding number of silver gulden, the silver gulden being calculated at 2 kroner, and replaces the bank with "legal means of payment".

Since the silver gulden contains much more silver than two one-crown pieces or even as a two-crown piece, and since the silver gulden are to be changed into coinage for the new coinage, then each of the two governments has a significant "coinage".

The actual supply of silver coins thus grows in this way.

How big the remainder of silver gulden remains then is unknown; they are still valid.

It is well known that inventories of talers in the German Reich have been turned into silver coins in exactly the same way, before the coins were wholly disregarded.

For the time before the outbreak of the war of 1914, the following picture emerges:

Austro-Hungarian monarchy.
Overview of the money types for July 1914.
(There are no optional money types, and there are no cash types that can be redeemed for gold.)

Österreichisch-ungarische Monarchie.
Übersicht der Geldarten für Juli 1914.

(Fakultative Geldarten gibt es nicht; es gibt auch keine in Goldgeld einlösbare Geldarten.)

Geldarten	Nach dem Annahmezwang	Nach der Entstehung	Nach der Zahlweise des Staates
1. Goldstücke zu 20 K und 10 K	} Kurantgeld	bares Geld	akzessor. Geld
2. Silbergulden zu 2 K	Kurantgeld	notales Geld	akzessor. Geld
3. Fünfkronenstücke (Silber)	} Scheidegeld I (bis 250 K)	notales Geld	akzessor. Geld
4. Zwei- und Einkronenstücke (Silber)	} Scheidegeld II (bis 50 K)	notales Geld	akzessor. Geld
5. Nickelmünzen zu 20 h und 10 h	} Scheidegeld III (bis 10 K)	notales Geld	akzessor. Geld
6. Bronzemünzen zu 2 h und 1 h	} Scheidegeld IV (bis 1 K)	notales Geld	akzessor. Geld
7. Banknoten zu 1000, 100, 50, 20 und 10 K	} Kurantgeld	notales Geld	valutar. Geld

Zu 2.: Silbergulden; der Münzfuß ist: aus 500 Gramm feinen Silbers werden 45 Silbergulden geschlagen; Feinheit des Münzsilbers 900/1000.

Zu 3.: Fünfkronenstücke; aus 1000 Gramm Münzsilber von der Feinheit 900/1000 werden 41²/₃ Stück geschlagen.

Zu 4.: Zwei- und Einkronenstücke; aus 1000 Gramm Münzsilber von der Feinheit 835/1000 werden 100 bzw. 200 Stück geschlagen.

[Redeemed for gold

By Money types
  By the acceptance obligation
  By Origin of the state
1. Gold piece 10 to 20 K currency cash money | accessory money
2. Silver gulden to 2 K currency nominal money | accessory money
3. 5 K silver nominal money | accessory money
4. 2 and 1 K silver nominal money | accessory money
5. Nickel 20 h and 10 h nominal money | accessory money (up to 10 K)
6. Bronze 2 h and 1 h nominal money | accessory money
7. Banknotes 1000, 100, 50, 20, 10 K currency nominal money valuta money

To 2 .: silver gulden; the coin base is: out of 500 grams of fine silver, 45 silver gulden are struck; Fineness of the coin silver 900/1000.

To 3 .: five-crown pieces; from 1000 grams of coin silver of the fineness 900/1000 are beaten 41 2/3 piece.

To 4 .: two- and one-crown pieces; from 1000 grams of coin silver from the fineness 835/1000 100 or 200 pieces are beaten.

If we compare retrospectively with the German money, as it was in July 1914, then it follows: In both fields of law, only gold is "hylic" metal, that is, only gold becomes unlimited, even for private account, coins marked, which are therefore referred to as cash.

The metals silver, nickel and copper are used here as well as there only to emergency coins.

The banknotes have general acceptance in the German Reich as well as in Austria-Hungary.

In contrast, the following differences exist:
In Austria, the silver gulden, the currency of the Exvalutary, but which has become necessary through the suspension of the unrestricted expression of silver (1879), is still in effect; In the German Empire, the

taler, which became an exvalutary in 1871, is no longer valid.

Jik Austria-Hungary has no optional money type; Reich treasury notes are optional in the German Reich.

In Austria-Hungary, there are no paper grades; In the German Reich, the Reich treasury notes are, so to speak, state notes of the Reich.

In Austria-Hungary, a much richer development was granted to the divisional money; There are four types and you can pay in divisional still payments up to 250 crowns; There are only two species in the German Empire and the upper limit for use is 20 Mk.

In Austria-Hungary there are no money types that can be redeemed in gold money; in the German Reich are the banknotes, the Reich treasury notes for amounts of more than 20 Mk., all silver coins in amounts of 200 Mk. and more, all nickel and copper coins in amounts of 50 Mk. and more, so all types of money, not are themselves gold money, redeemable in gold.

But the most significant difference is: Value money is the gold coins in Germany; In the Austro-Hungarian monarchy, on the other hand, banknotes are valutary money.

The regulation of the intervalutary courses against the gold countries takes place in Austria-Hungary by special institutions, which are not developed in the German Reich in the same degree. -

II. The innovations to be discussed in the business operations of the bank were greatly facilitated by a measure which Dr. med. Leon Ritter von Bilinski, at that time Governor, reported in a lecture, which was held in Krakow on 2 October 1906 at the Polish Juristentage. From a publication about it we extract excerpts:

The gold holdings of the two governments are most significant; they are almost exclusively from customs duties; From this source, 100 million kroner annually go to the two governments together. In the past, these funds were borrowed from private banks, which had the duty, in return for a low return, to make available to each government, in due time, the sums required for their payments abroad. That the banks deserved to do business with this business is fine; but that they were participating in profitable international speculation with government funds and that they charged the governments excessively high rates for the foreign currencies seemed less in order. The governments, as it were, relied on the grace and disfavour of the private banks.

In the years 1900 and 1901, the finance ministers of both governments and the highest officials of the bank met for a consultation which took place in Ischl, in the house of Governor L. von Bilinski, on 8 August 1901.

In doing so, the two finance ministers (von Böhm-Bawerk and Lukács) undertook "to transfer in the future all their gold receipts to the administration of the bank and to have their international payments made by them (ie by the bank)."

The Bank, on the other hand, assumed the obligation to pay interest on these gold holdings and, on the other hand, to manage them. At the same time it was suggested on this occasion that the bank - without obligation by law - put gold coins in the domestic traffic.

The first question to be asked is: what does it mean that the bank - as it is usually called - has experimentally "put gold coins into circulation"?

Above all, it does not mean unlimited redemption of the notes in gold coins. The bank is not obliged to do this; it is only envisaged as the ultimate goal of the reform for an as yet unknown date in the future (§83), but this paragraph is provisionally suspended under §111 of the Banking Act. An obligation of this kind is still missing.

However, it would be conceivable that the bank would voluntarily be prepared for such a redemption of the notes, that is to say the so-called optional redemption - without legal coercion in addition - had set in motion.

But there is also no optional redemption in unlimited amounts to any request of the clientele.

The Bank's measure to "put pieces of gold in circulation" is quite another and has nothing to do with redeeming the notes.

From the extremely instructive treatise of Alexander Spitzmüller, "The Austro-Hungarian Currency Reform" (Journal of Economics, Volume XI, Vienna 1902, p. 506, or in the special imprint, Vienna 1902, p. 63) one learns about the following: "Since the end of April In 1901, golden twenty-crown pieces and, since the end of October 1901, also gold ten-crown pieces were put to the test for the following reason: one wanted to determine approximately how much of these coins would be kept in circulation.

So the attempt was made how many gold coins were needed to bring about the state of saturation of the traffic with gold. The Bank had a considerable interest in gaining experience of this future time when the unconditional redemption of the notes should take place in gold, for their stock of cash had to be greater or smaller, to the minimum, depending on that saturation much or little gold coins required. But what does "putting into circulation" mean?

It does not mean redemption of offered notes, but it means giving gold coins to other payments made by the bank. More precisely: the bank has to make a payment; notes of 20 and 10 crowns should also be used, according to earlier usage; these notes (not all notes) now hold them back, using the golden twenty- and ten-crown pieces instead.
So here's no mention of grades that would have been handed over for redemption.
Rather, it was a process of exploring the measure of popularity enjoyed by people in the Monarchy.

The success was surprising; it had been expected that a much larger amount of gold coins would be "in circulation" than it was the case.

When comparing the exit and entrance of the gold coins to find the "balance," it turned out (according to Spitzmüller, op. Cit.):
Until September 30, 1902 gold coins had gone out more than received:

127007940 kroner.
This amount would be about sufficient to saturate the traffic with gold coins.

From another source one learns of this most remarkable experiment, that this balance grew strongly over the years until 1905, and that from then on it diminished again:
State gold coins were put into circulation on balance:

on December 31, 1901. , , , 55 486 760 crowns
" September 30, 1902. , , , 127 007 940 "
" December 31, 1902. , , , 133 301 460 "
" December 31, 1903. , , , 159 037 470 "
" December 31, 1904. , , , 210 382 010 "
" December 31, 1905. , , , 291 221 590 "
" December 31, 1906. , , , 255 195520 "
" December 31, 1907. , , , 234 763 200 "
" December 31, 1908. , , , 214 594 400 "
" December 31, 1909. , , , 224 730 510 "
" June 30, 1910. , , , , , , , , 223 833 050 "

According to J. von Gruber, Lieutenant Governor of the Bank, the balance at the end of December 1911 was 253.8 million crowns and arose as follows:
until then, the bank had spent 2,193.8 million crowns in those gold coins; and collected. , , , , , , , 1,939.9 "
so there was a net issue of , , , , 253.9 million crowns (almost as above).

(See the article in the "Neue Freie Presse" of 2 August 1912, "The Monetary Policy in the Last Twenty Years.")

Thus, out of every 100 crowns marketed in the manner described, about 88 crowns are again returned to the bank and only 12 kroner remained in circulation. It was seen that gold coins are not very popular unless there is a premium. -

However, this strange attempt is not quite as harmless as it looks, for indeed 253.9 million crowns are in circulation in gold coins, where - because the formation of an agio is otherwise prevented - they are of no use whatsoever. Should warlike times occur, which is always to be feared in the neighborhood of the Balkans, the owners of those pieces of gold will by no means hurry to pay them to the bank for notes; Rather, they will invest hidden treasures and hope for agio profit. That should have been countered by those attempts.

Only those who have the complete acceptance of the cash payment - as the government of both states does - for the inevitable. The goal of the monetary reform of 1892 can consider that attempt to be flawless and, as it were, self-evident. Of course, this attempt succeeded in the sense of its authors only because of other measures the Goldagio had already been eliminated. -

III. With regard to the payment of customs duties, the government adopted a measure of major importance on 30 November 1900. It still remains permissible for the customs payer to obtain any kind of Austrian gold coins or even gold pieces from France or those from the German Reich, in order to apply them in the manner described at the customs offices. But if he does not want to do so, a new way will be opened for him by turning to the bank to buy so-called tariff gold orders. This is to be understood.

It is not necessary to pay the customs duties at the customs offices, but can direct the payment to the bank, with the order that the bank issue a tariff gold instruction, directed to the order of the central government; This instruction is paid by the customs official at the customs office, instead of the gold money. The state gets, as it were, then the gold money at the bank, or disposes of it at will.

After the work: XXXVII. regular annual meeting of the General Assembly of the Austro-Hungarian Bank, on February 8, 1918, Vienna, page XXIV, customs gold orders were issued:
in 1914 for. , , 68.5 million crowns

"" 1915 ". , , , ,54.5 "
"" 1916 ". , , , ,57.3 "
"" 1917 ". , , , ,27.4 "
This greatly facilitates the cashier service at the customs offices.

The question then arises: in what way does the man who orders a tariff gold instruction from the bank pay for it?

If this man physically deposits the allowable gold coins with the bank, then the bank does nothing more than cash transactions for the state. This may happen here and there.

But now comes the main thing: the applicant for a tariff gold instruction can deposit at the bank also notes of the Austro-Hungarian bank. This is what the printed description of banking transactions, called "lessons", says.
If, for example, the amount of the duty is 1000 kroner, then how many crowns in banknotes does that customer have to pay? Does he pay 1000 crowns in notes or does he pay more?

He pays 1000 crowns in notes; he acquires the tariff gold instruction "al pari". These two Italian words are used in the already mentioned article by Ignaz von Gruber in the "Neue Freie Presse" of 2 and 3 August 1912.

From this, however, two things follow: First, even then there was a way to pay the tariffs in grades at no extra charge; quite logically, since the agio of the gold coins was known to have disappeared. Only one had to choose the detour of the tariff gold instruction.

Second, the tariff gold instruction obliges the bank to deliver the gold money to the state or its orders, or to write it well for the time being, while the bank received the amount in its own notes.

This is a big surprise, because you can see immediately: in this business - not in general - the bank is ready to cash in its notes in gold coins. In this business, therefore, we have redemption of the notes, not only in "sounding coin" - because even the silver sounds - but in cash, in our, narrow sense.

Thus, while a general redemption of the notes in cash money does not take place at all, it does, however, intervene in customs transactions insofar as the bank is used as a mediator. -

IV. The regulation of the inter-valutary rates, as operated by the bank, can be described much more accurately according to recent publications.

It remains that in this activity the reason for the fixed exchange rates lay (up to the war of 1914); but it would be wrong to call that activity simply a foreign exchange policy: that is far too narrow! Foreign exchange policy is one of them, but it is not enough and has only been the first measure in this direction.

In Vienna, those bills that are payable abroad are called foreign exchange. One learns now from a book: "Die Agioreferve der öfterreichifch-ungarifchen Bank", in 4°, Vienna 1898, whose author (Friedrich Schmid, he was Deputy Secretary General in 1908), a bank official, on the title is not mentioned about this Matter (p. 123): "The bank's trade in currencies and currencies has only recently become more important and of particular importance to the money market; The bank absorbs the currencies and foreign exchange offered to it on falling foreign exchange rates and gives them back on demand when the prices rise. The purpose of these transactions is to keep the value of the Austrian currency as stable as possible in relation to the gold, and possibly to prevent the formation of a Gold agio; the Bank, therefore, seeks, through this business, as long as it is not cash-bearing, to achieve the purpose which, in the case of a cash-paying bank, is achieved by the cash redemption of the notes in gold. For profit, these businesses are not undertaken. If this were the case, the bank would have to seek to pay its foreign currency and currency at the highest possible prices in order to obtain the greatest possible benefit from the difference between the purchase price and the selling price, but it does the opposite. Their purpose is to prevent the formation of high foreign exchange rates."

A. Spitzmüller (see above, p. 57 of the special edition, p. 500 of the journal) provides information on the date: It happened at the beginning of 1894 by the Austrian Minister of Finance von Plener and the Hungarian Finance Minister Wekerle. The Bank "designed the foreign exchange business, especially in the period 1897-1900, in a way that is isolated in the history of the central bank and ... in banking, the most vivid interest to raise is appropriate ".

A few lines later, it says: By that measure, the bank has actually accepted the cash payment to foreign countries; Any nervousness in the market, in terms of inter-valutary exchange rates with gold countries, has disappeared, and there is reasonable hope of preserving this condition.

No doubt, then, that the importance of the matter was recognized; On the other hand, a more detailed description was lacking, and there was silence on highly important details until the highly commendable article by J. von Gruber (in the Neue Freie Presse, 2 and 3 August 1912) appeared. This clearly shows that the Austro-Hungarian Bank seeks to deprive foreign bankers of money from private bankers, to concentrate them on themselves and, above all, to eliminate speculation that has been found to be detrimental to the exchange-rate courses.

But this is not done by currency trading alone, but by trade in all kinds of means of payment which can be made in the foreign country in question. If, for example, Germany were in question, it would be necessary to affix: German gold coins; Bills of exchange, due in Germany; Checks, if the Austro-Hungarian bank maintains credit there; finally gold bars (including foreign coins) because of their convertibility into German gold coins.

Further, it is important: the bank does not blindly drive this trade in foreign means of payment (in the wider sense of the word) to any customer who contacts, but picks its people; So there is a kind of commercial police in the game. The bank wants to know whether the customer wants to acquire the means of payment only in order to solve obligations, which originate from solid commercial transactions; or if he is a value speculator, for example, who then should not enjoy any promotion of his purposes. This distinction requires a great deal of personal knowledge. But, according to Walter Federn, another means is in use: he who desires means of payment of a later date has the presumption that he is in charge of a "legitimate" business; while cash with an immediate due date is suspected of serving a speculation. In any case, the clientele is screened out.

After agreeing with the customer on the type of coveted payment, the question of the price comes into consideration. J. von Gruber (supra) says: the bank gives away these means of payment "at a price which, according to the statutory provisions mentioned above, it is not allowed to raise far from coin parity".

So not far from the coin parity; but a little higher; perhaps so high that the bank can re-acquire the funds tendered without sacrifices.

However, this regulation of the inter-valutary rates against the gold countries now does almost the same thing as if general cash redemption of the notes took place. Therefore, Spitzmüller says a. a. O., as it were "accepted the cash payment to foreign countries," meaning that the bank delivers foreign currency at almost fixed rates.

Incidentally, the bank's intervention described above represents a major change in the market for third-party means of payment: **it is no longer the competition of many banks and the indiscriminate admission of all customers, but the concentration at the Austro-Hungarian bank and its supervision of the nature of the business - a kind of censorship - makes itself felt; whereby the central bank receives more and more official duties - in addition to business.**

Since the course fortification had already had a success from then on in 1896, so in 1911 there was a series of 16 calendar years in which the regulation of the Intervalutary courses, at first against Germany, had succeeded.

This explains why, when the statutes of the Austro-Hungarian Bank were renewed, one dared to take an unprecedented step. Those course regulation, before only voluntarily undertaken by the bank, is declared by the law of 8 August 1911 as a duty of the bank. The Bank, along with its other duties, is an office charged with exchange control, with the threat that a loss of privilege will occur as soon as the Bank is unable to perform the task.

Such a provision has not yet been in any bank statute.

In the work of J. Raudnitz, the Austrian monetary and banking laws, Vienna 1912, the statutes of the Austro-Hungarian Bank are printed.
Page 289 can be found in Title I, Article 1, in the third paragraph:
"The Austro-Hungarian Bank is obliged, by all means at its disposal, to ensure that the value of its notes expressed in the course of foreign bills remains permanently secured in accordance with the parity of the legal base of the crown currency."

Page 337 can be found in Title XIII, Article 111, in the second paragraph (the "mean time" means the time until the notes are redeemable):
"In the meantime, if the Austro-Hungarian Bank does not fulfill its obligation to use all means at its disposal to ensure that the value of its notes as expressed in the foreign exchange rate remains constant, in accordance with the parity of the legal base of the Crown currency (Article 1), except in the case of a temporary removal of the Austro-Hungarian Bank from both sides of the monarchy, which has been legally enacted, this will result in the forfeiture of the privilege, except in cases of force majeure both governments recognized immediate prevention. "

The two passages came into the statutes by the law of August 8, 1911.

The wording of Article 1 is very striking. At first, the term "foreign change" is quite vague; Obviously, the legislator has thought primarily of Germany, and perhaps of other gold-currency countries, and he will say that as long as the gold currency exists in those countries in the strictest sense of the word, the notes of the Austro-Hungarian bank on the stock exchange of those countries should not lower (ie those foreign means of payment in Vienna are not higher) than the coin parity indicates.

It does not seem to have been thought that the Austrian grades could sometimes be higher. For this, however, unlikely case, the bank seems to be obliged to no regulatory intervention, although it is not excluded by the wording.
Likewise, it is not thought that the gold standard may fall into decay in foreign countries. What happens then?

Finally, it is strange that the price of Austrian notes is simply called their "value"; the judgment of the foreign country is thus called authoritative.

These uncertainties could have been avoided if it had been said that the bank must make every effort to ensure that the Austrian gold coins did not receive a premium on the Vienna Stock Exchange, or, more precisely, that they did not receive a premium that went beyond the border. In any case, this goal would be achieved by redeeming the notes in cash, which is out of the question, since the cash payment is rejected; but it would also be achieved if the bank, after its custom since 1904, provides the means of payment of the gold countries at nearly fixed prices corresponding to the coin pari: then foreign countries no longer attract Austrian gold coins, because, from there Austria behaves as if it had cash-on-pay.

The success of Austrian price regulation continued even after the law of 1911 almost into the last days of July 1914, as can be seen from the following prices, which were listed on the Berlin Stock Exchange;

There, according to the Frankfurter Zeitung of July 28, 1914, they paid for 100 crowns, whose coin parity is 85 Mk.
on March 31, 1914. , , , , 85.25 Mk.

"April 30, 1914. , , , , 85,025 "
"May 30, 1914. , , , , , 84.85 "
"June 30, 1914. , , , , , 84.55 "
"July 23, 1914. , , , , , 84.525 "
"July 24. 1914. , , , , , 84.45 "
"July 25. 1914. , , , , , 84.225 "
"July 27. 1914. , , , , , 84.225 "

So it was, since 1906 - for a period of about 18 years - the course fortification succeeded and would probably have continued to succeed if the peace had been preserved in Europe; but it turned out differently.

Almost at the moment when the new banking constitution, which had hitherto only actually practiced course regulation, became a legal institution, it repeated itself what had happened in 1859 and 1866: the outbreak of war shook the newly-founded work and completely destroyed it.

But this has also happened in the neighboring countries and must therefore not be attributed to the Austrian system as it existed in 1914.

A monetary system that could resist such a shock does not exist.

When all the usual trade relations are broken, and when states are forced to choose the most desperate means to save their existence, all the preconditions of an orderly monetary system sink there. Then there is nothing left but a currency of emergency without all course regulation, as it has already been experienced after April 1859 and after May 1866. A healing is not to be thought of earlier than after the peace.

For the time after the war, however, the same tasks come into view as in the earlier accidents, and for that Austria will always remain instructive.

§ 20. Understanding about monetary value and prices

An old saying goes: the truth is more the result of error than of confusion. The term money value, if it occurs without addition, so to speak money value in itself, is a completely unclear term with which nothing at all can be. Wherever it is used, it only causes mischief. We want to think about that by looking at it below.

Wherever value is involved, it is a comparison. This is nothing new, because in § 8 of Schopenhauer's "Basis of Morality" one reads the apt words: "Every value is a comparative quantity, and even it is necessary in a double relation: for in the first place, it is relative, meaning for someone and, secondly, it is comparative in that it is a comparison with something else that it is valued for. Beyond these two relations, value loses all meaning and meaning. "Again and again, however, it is forgotten. So almost all people think that there is a monetary value in itself; This so-called monetary value does not exist. So we do not say that the money in any sense has any value; it can have value in many ways. But it makes no sense to ask for the value of money unless the meaning of this question is explained beforehand. We want to give first information about the confusion prevailing here.

Certainly it is that the State Theory of Money does not participate in the confusion; it often has to do with questions about the value of money in some sense, for example, it asks about the value of the currency of a foreign state; or it is asked about the value of an accessory money of our own state; or according to the value of a synchartal kind of money which belongs to our state and to a foreign state at the same time.

On the other hand is occasionally talked about gold values with us or the silver values with us. But in all these cases, it is clear that we have a certain reference stock in mind, and that is our valuta money. Of a monetary value in itself, with a mention of the comparison good, we never talk.

Economics is different from the State Theory of Money. Our

economists talk a great deal about monetary value without adding, and think of other questions than those mentioned above; these are "prices," as is most fully expressed, and there is now quite unmistakably some confusion, because the incomplete expression of the value of money can be supplemented in various ways. This could happen in the following way:

I. The economist thinks of a particular commodity, examines the prices paid for that commodity in and in the country in which and in the period, and uses statistics to determine the mean price of that commodity. As examples one could imagine: cereals, or certain metals or even more closely certain precious metals. The result would then always be of the following kind: the price of the chosen good was on average for the unit of measure, and so many units of value of that country and of that time. The payment has existed in the valutary money type, which always appears as money par excellence.

Now comes the decisive step: our economist reverses the relationship that is statistically found between that good and the money and says: If that good is chosen as the basis of the judgment and the question is posed according to the value of the money, then the result is: 100 Marks at that time were worth x units of the commodity over which the statistical examination of the prices took place.
One should, however, note and hold that this way of determining the value of money is based on a reversal of the mutual relationship between commodity and means of payment.
What used to be goods is thought of as a means of payment, and what was previously a means of payment is thought of as a commodity.

Nobody can be denied to do this reversal of relationships in thought; but whoever wants to do it has to say it, and above all he has to name the estate he bases. Only then does the reader know and can comment on the matter. -

Supposing that there were two statistical studies of the price, for two different periods, but in the same country, it would perhaps emerge for the commodity under investigation that the average price had changed, let us assume in the ratio of 12 to 13. This good would have become more expensive for each unit of quantity. Then, when that reversal of relations is made, the statement about money must be: after that examination of the good, one gets the impression that the value of money has diminished; You now have to apply 13 value units where previously only 12 were needed. There is nothing wrong with this; Anyone who calculates so must wait to see whether the reader wants to recognize this judgment as sufficient about the value of money in every respect; but if that good is recognized as authoritative, then the matter is settled. How one wants to compel the reader to approve the choice of the good, one does not see. The calculator thus remains uncertain whether he finds his statistical applause with respect to the "value of money in every respect".

In the state theory of money this consideration does not belong. The state presupposes - on all occasions where prices are concerned - to use units of value that are legally customary, and that payments are made in valuta money.

What comes out, for example, through a statistical price investigation, does not have the slightest legal effect. The state knows no variability "of the monetary value". The moment the state pronounces the validation of the plays, he says that existing debts can be redeemed with these pieces; new debts too, and it is assumed for new debts that the contracting parties will retain their advantage.

The economist may, however, make price investigations and exchange the concepts of commodity and money. It is then only a particularly emphatic way to inform the reader about changes in average prices by saying - to follow the above example - it is just as if the value of money were reduced, which meant, however, that it should be invalidated. "It's just as if," these words are easily taken by the reader in a more serious sense! Namely in the sense that the legal validity of the pieces has changed - and that is certainly not the case.

II. So far we have only talked about a single good whose price changes would have been statistically analyzed.

But there is another kind of investigation: a number of goods are selected, which must be natural, for example: wheat, coals, important metals such as iron, copper, and the like. So we arrange a complex of goods, as we call it, and examine statistically how the price of this complex has changed. Before this can happen, however, it must be said what quantities of each good included in the complex should be considered, for example, one kilogram of wheat, one ton of coal, one pound of platinum, etc. It does not matter which amounts one takes from each good, but an agreement on the quantities is certainly necessary for the purpose of the complex of goods to be clearly determined. If this uniqueness of the complex is reached, the statistical investigation of the price of our complex can take place, but not before. Now, for two periods, the examination of the price should be carried out statistically; then one receives for the first period a number of value units, for example x_1 marks; for the second period also a number of value units, for example x_2 marks. These numbers are known as index numbers. If the later index number, that is, x_2, is greater than the earlier index, that is, greater than x_1, then the value of that complex has increased; in the opposite case, the value of the complex has fallen. There can be no doubt about that.

The statisticians who compute such index numbers, however, do not stand by this undoubted fact, but they go further by saying: One sees from it that "the value of the money" has moved in reverse, like the index numbers. If the index number has grown, it is clear that the value of the money has fallen; on the other hand, the value of money has increased when the index number has become smaller.

Here, the same psychological process prevails that we have previously established: **our statistician considers money as the thing whose value is to be found, and the commodity complex as the thing with which to compare the money.**

Before, when determining the price, but the goods have been compared with the money. So our statistician has switched the relationship between commodity and money: he places the money where the commodity stood.

The correct mode of expression would be obvious: the change in the price of the chosen complex has taken place as if the value of money (more correctly, the validity of the piece) had changed so and so. Instead, he says: the value of money has changed. He conceals that it depends on whether the goods complex is granted as authoritative and pretends that this is beyond doubt; and he further assumes that his "value of money" is the same as the validity of the play. But the reader has forgotten that he must recognize the complex of commodities as authoritative, and has further forgotten that validity, as a legal notion, is quite independent of what one can buy with money.

Index numbers can therefore say nothing about the legal nature of money, therefore, do not belong in the state theory of money. They belong to economics, and even here they mean nothing more than a change in the language of price statistics; they do not deliver anything new, but only say the old in a different form. They show that commodity prices can change, which no one has doubted; and put it this way: the change has taken place as if the money had changed its validity so and so. But it does not follow that the validity has changed!

However, the general possibility of commodity prices changing alters much; namely the position of the interest of those who own money and those who own goods. But this is a matter of itself. It almost seems as if many writers proceeded on the assumption that the goods, each for themselves, would normally have a fixed price, which changes abnormally every now and then - which, after all, can not be at issue.

Above all, however, index calculators must be reminded that they simply do not offer anything else than highly welcome news about price changes. Some of them believe that they have found something else, a process of change on the side of money, an "increase or decrease in value" which, they do not doubt, affects the price changes of goods. This is an unheard of circularity! The change of value of money which they determine is derived only from the statistics of prices: how is the price change of the goods - to be explained from the change in the price of goods?

III. But what about when we consider the income of the economic persons?

There are people who receive their annual income in fixed amount; That includes officials, whether public or private, whose numbers are so great in Germany and whose influence on sentiment is so important. The man with a fixed salary so easily complains of the fading of the value of money when the price increases. what does he mean with that?

Such a man surveys his situation and calculates so: I spend so much for dwelling, so much for food, so much for my children's tuition, etc. I used to keep a thousand marks a year, but I can barely make debts. So "the monetary value" has changed a lot to my detriment. -

Apparently that man has formed a "complex" of goods; Food, Apartment Rental, Beer and Wine, Tobacco etc. He has, from his expenditure book, set in this complex in addition to the prices, and finds his index number greatly enlarged against earlier years: so for him the monetary value has changed greatly, and to his detriment. He expects us to be very precise.

But his neighbor, who forms such a complex, also finds an index number - but another; because one smokes, the other does not do it; one travels a lot, the other travels a little, and so on. For him, therefore, the monetary value may also be changed, but not in the same way. A match does not arise.

The only result of this investigation is that price increases on the goods consumed by the official place a heavy burden on him, and he can argue that he needs allowance. But he can not assert that evil is due to money in itself; we have only one special case of the index calculation in front of us. He has only described his interest, which is affected by the price increase. But where is it written that his life situation must remain the same? his contract is a fixed sum of the annual income in money. He is now annoyed by the inflation, his income is no longer enough for him - but it is not the constitution of the financial system, but the nature of our economic traffic. -

But there are also people whose income comes about in a completely different way. Think of the farmers, the owners of coal mines or iron works, in short, the producers of goods. Their income is first in their products, which they put up for sale. Every year, the farmer produces so much wheat, which he produces in pits, so to speak, and so many hundred pounds of iron or coal. These goods must be sold before a money income forms for him. If this man forms his goods complex and calculates what his index number is, he finds - with rising prices - that this number increases. But since he does not buy the goods he has set, but sells them, the change is for salvation.

Whoever acts only as a consumer of goods, as the official does, harms the price increase; Anyone who only acts as a producer benefits them. Anyone who acts as a consumer of certain goods and at the same time as a producer of other goods may experience damage, or perhaps benefit.

The economic analysis must cover both cases. Price increases shift the interests according to the class to which the economic person belongs.

The interests of the classes are a matter of great importance - but they have nothing to do with the constitution of the money, which is described in the State Theory of Money.

IV. Also, merchants and commercial entrepreneurs often speak of expensive money or cheap if they work with outside funds, that is, if they have taken out loans to increase their business. Especially at the contractor, this case is common. When asked why his buildings are standing still, he replies that the money is too expensive or even says that the value of the money is now too high. But if the business goes fast, it is often explained that the money is cheap now, as some say: the money is of no great value now. What everyone here means, everyone sees: they talk about the interest conditions that have to be approved in order to obtain a loan in money. It should be made clearer: now I have to grant too high interest on loans; or now the interest demands for loans have become lower.

Anyone who speaks of high or low monetary value instead blurs all differences again; for here there is no talk of a definite good (for instance of wheat or silver), nor of an agreed upon complex of goods, as in the cases previously discussed. But it is asked what fraction (how many percent) of the capital one must pay annually to the lender. This is something else! How can you summarize such fundamentally different things under the same name "value of money"! The result is a hopeless confusion that gives the beginner the impression that there is a deep secret hidden behind the "values of money" that awaits solution.
The solution is obvious: one has selected an indistinct, because incomplete, expression for many phenomena which, when considered individually and fully described, are by no means puzzling. It has created a problem by creating confusion! -

If the German in 1917 says: Our money has lost on the stock exchanges of neutral countries in value - expressed in the local money - he is right and it is issued to our economists the call to explain this by the disturbed trade relations.

Moreover, if the German says, "Many prices have risen inland, compared with the state of 1913, he is also right, and it is up to our economists to prove what disturbances in the inner market are to blame.

If the German says: "The construction of houses stands still, because mortgage loans only come about under harsh conditions, this is quite true; The economist must now explain to him why higher interest rates are now demanded for such loans than before.

But to explain all this for one single reason by the misty expression "the value of money has diminished" - is, to put it mildly, no explanation, but negligence.

Needless to say, the phrase of the diminished purchasing power of money is equally incapable of explaining anything; it states only with altered words that inflation prevails and does not even do it properly, since it suggests that all prices have changed to the same extent, which is not true at all.

What should one finally say, if one must read: that a satisfactory constitution of money among others should grant: immutability of the monetary value. What do you mean by that? Maybe firmness of the inter-valutary courses? If yes, against which country? Or firmness of "prices"? Which prices?
Or always the same behavior against noble metals? And against which of these metals?

Here, obviously, all certainty of the concepts is missing - for which, however, there is a kind of consolation. All insights develop gradually. As the child plays with the kit and only the man really builds, terms are first spoken back and forth before questions are solved. We have already reached the lowest level - maybe we'll carry it on.

Here the opponents of state theory could rejoice: "we said it at once, one does not know there to give information about the monetary value".

Certainly not; no rational theory can answer an unreasonably asked question. Our theory can show, however, that the question of the monetary value in itself, without further details, is unreasonable. Who nevertheless feels called to answer such a question, may he do so; but he has nothing in common with us. That the common man summarizes all his feelings about inflation under the heading of diminished monetary value, is true, but can decide nothing.

Also, some teachers will long remain baffling the beginner by promising him revelations about the value of money itself; There are also among the scholars - mood people! And how appealing is the boundless value problem for them!

V. But now an opponent could object: two facts remain undeniable. During the war, and even more after that, tremendous upheavals in the prices of almost all goods and almost all services have occurred. On the other hand, everyone sees the masses of paper money newly created and marketed. Should not these two things be related? Then changes on the side of money would be responsible for the overthrow of the prices.

This idea is hard to eradicate; For it meets the need of the layman to deduce everything for a single reason. But let's be careful!

It is indeed the job of the economists to examine the financial economy of the state and to tell us whether the monstrous expenditure incurred by the state through the growth of warriors can be solved in another way than through the creation of paper money, better of emergency money low value or worthless substances. So far, you have not been able to have any other means than this, which does not occur alone, but always in addition to other means. But this is a task of public finance, which understands the state as an economic person. In the state theory of money this question does not belong; Here the state is conceived only as an authority, which arranges the payment system according to the legal side. The economist must, however, know about this legal content before undertaking that task of finance science. But then he still has much to do, because he has the task of observation, since the schematic answers from the vocabulary of the so-called theory are no longer sufficient. Some examples may clarify this.

As the war approaches, on the inside of the ramparts of its fortresses, the state builds extensive buildings in which hundreds of workers make cartridges. Very high wages are offered and paid for in newly created paper money. The servants have not yet achieved similar earnings; they announce their reign, enter the cartridge factory, and in a few weeks the wages of the servants in the city are doubled. Here the state has revolutionized economic conditions through its behavior; He still does it in other cases, and we hope to hear that from the Economist.

But more. The disturbance does not necessarily come from the state.

Let's face the railways. The numerous masses of employees working for the railways join forces for common action; their leaders command that higher wages are to be demanded, refusing to continue working. This appearance succeeds: the managing authority must increase the fares twice, in threefold. Is this due to the money constitution?

Is not it possible for every monetary system to shift the balance of power of the economic parties and to produce enormous price changes?

Just think back to the experiences at the outbreak of the war: the state buys up all the horses that can be obtained: it buys all the automobiles that it finds in private homes; he orders endless masses of ammunition; He employs all weapon factories through new orders, he uses all means of transport, especially the railways; he buys food for millions of soldiers. The state pays and salaries to the troops deployed in the war. Can he do all this without paper money?

Certainly not. And if he does - does not he disturb all existing production relations?

And further: where does the state take all the teams that it summons? He deprives them of the commercial life; the miners step out of their service, the factory workers become soldiers, the workers of the small industry are called up; the farmer leaves his farm, the farm laborers carry weapons. The manufacturer, the craftsman, the merchant, in short all employed persons are deprived of their former activity and are in the field. The whole bourgeois life is undermined: and there are "the prices" to remain undisturbed? But above all: that is to blame for the creation of paper money? The war compels us to change the usual bourgeois life, and the paper money is only the means to carry out the forced revolution. It's a curious limitation to just sue the paper money. The far more important task of the economist would be to describe the nature of the disturbances and to illuminate the ways of the financial economy.

Nobody ever denied that this had to happen next to the state theory of money; but without this theory, it can not happen.

Attachment.

The literature about the state theory of money

The following are cited: First, the smaller publications of the author, insofar as they relate to monetary matters; secondly, the treatises from the author of the political science seminar on Strasbourg, also only insofar as they deal with money; and third, the judgments on the State Theory of Money, published in books or magazines, as far as they have become known to the author.

Completeness can not be guaranteed; in particular, of the many articles in newspapers, only a few could be mentioned. -

The judgments were very unfavorable in the beginning, even those made orally, and even if they were from a friendly side. The author was offered the prospect that his book would have no effect whatsoever, and that perhaps decades later it would be unearthed by an ambitious literary historian as a sign of an outrageous aberration.

The first printed advertisements (by A. Voigt and by W. Lotz) were also quite negative and were noted with satisfaction by A. Wagner.

Only W. Lexis spoke with caution and usual modesty.

The earliest lively approval comes from Dr. L. Calligaris, who worked as an official in the Austro-Hungarian Bank in Vienna and had written about the Austrian monetary system. He quite paid off to the practitioners and wrote three essays below, along with many newspaper articles, to make room for state theory. He suffered severely during the war and died on 14 September 1920.

Another practitioner, Dr. Friedrich Bendixen, director of the mortgage bank in Hamburg, has shown full understanding of the state theory, has adequately defended it and made it widely accessible. The appearance of this brilliant writer has become more comprehensible through an obituary published by a friend of his, Max M. Warburg, in the Bank Archive (XIXth Year, No. 22, 15 August 1920). Thereafter, Bendixen was born on September 30, 1864; he died on July 29, 1920.

I personally knew him only a little; He visited me twice in Strasbourg, each time only for a few hours.

Bendixen was a passionate letter writer and replaced the lack of personal contact with peers with truly inexhaustible communications, always in the finest form and with a cordial attitude. He had the correspondence with me collected and copied in typescript; There were seven issues, together 818 folio pages.

One does not think that I was the instructing part of this; the driving force was rather he: it emerged from the practitioner by force of writers. He was particularly keen to put economic considerations at the side of government considerations. This has been very stimulating to younger forces, and Bendixen has even from a distance, by correspondence, even students produced, for example, in his last year of life the author of the work "The Soul of Money", Jena 1920, 370 pages, Government Councilor Karl Elster who reports about it in his preface; he too is one of the most zealous defenders of state theory.

Of those who were my disciples, which is certainly not the case with the latter, merit has been considerable. Alfred Schmidt-Essen, by numerous articles in the press, as well as by his writing: "Valuta-Fibel, Jena 1921, 96 pages; and dr. Kurt Singer by the writing: "The money as a sign", Jena 1920, 206 pages. -

See postscript page 461.

I. Writings of the author concerning monetary matters.

1. G. F. Knapp, Vereinstaler Austrian character (Vereinstaler öfterreichifchen Gepräges). Article in the "Frankfurter Zeitung" of October 19, 1900, second morning sheet, p. 3; short note.

2. --- Explanations to the state theory of money (Erläuterungen zur Staatlichen Theorie des Geldes).
Schmollers Yearbook, vol. XXX, 4th issue, 1906, pp. 381-393.
Content: The so-called "good with fixed value". - The so-called "purchasing power of money". - The nature of Assignaten-danger. - The real trouble with unredeemable paper money. - The crookedness of the

criticism. - Postscript about W. Lexis.

3. --- The legal historical foundations of the monetary system (Die rechtshiſtoriſchen Grundlagen des Geldweſens).
Schmollers Yearbook, Vol. XXX, 3rd Edition, 1906, pp. 45-60.
(Public lecture, held in Stuttgart on April 18, 1906,
at the IX. Assembly of German Historians; see. about that:
Historische Vierteljahrsschrift, 1906, p. 297.)

4. --- Coinage and money (Münzweſen und Geldweſen). Historic Quarter Jahrschrift, 1906, pp. 433-434; short note.

5. G. F. Knapp, The high discount rates and our constitution of the monetary system (Die hohen Diskontoſätze und unſere Verfaſſung des Geldweſens). Bank-Archiv, 4th year, No. 4 of 15 Nov. 1906, p. 41-44. This essay is in the present third edition of the State Theory of Money as § 18c. (Page 346).

6. --- The monetary question, viewed from the state (Die Währungsfrage, vom Staate aus betrachtet). Schmollers Yearbook, Vol. XXXI, 4th Edition, 1907, pp. 59-70. (Rectorate speech, held May 1, 1907.)
Content: It is not really the material (gold, silver, paper), but facilities for fixing the exchange rate against important neighboring countries. Today's gold standard serves this purpose, but inside the country more money than is necessary is put into circulation; Notable money would be enough for circulation, especially since central banks are starting to regulate exchange rates.

7. --- The relations of Austria to the state theory of money (Die Beziehungen Öſterreichs zur Staatlichen Theorie des Geldes). Journal of Economics, Social Policy and Administration, Vol. XVII, 1908, pp. 439-452. (Also reprinted in the Volkswirtschafts-Wochenschrift by Alexander Dorn.) Lecture held on March 24, 1908 at the 172st Plenary Assembly of the Assembly of Austrian Economists.

8. --- Money theory, State (Geldtheorie, Staatliche). Article in the

Handwörterbuch der Staatswissenschaften, edited by J. Conrad, etc., third edition, Vol. IV, 1909, pp. 610-618.

9. --- About the theories of money (über die Theorien des Geldweſens). Schmollers Yearbook, Vol. XXXIII, 2nd Edition, 1909, pp. 1-16. Lecture, held in the Legal Society of Leipzig on Dec. 30th. 1908, under the presidencies of the Reichsgerichtsrat Hermann Dietz. -
Content: Two types of theoreticians: programmatic and analyzing. - The main thing is the administrative order of the monetary system with the political objectives of fixing the inter-valutary courses. - The international treaties actually want to be pari contracts. - Austria dropped the pari-plan of 1857; Italy has realized the pari-idea of the Latin Coin Confederation.

10. --- About the monetary value and its changes (über den Geldwert und ſeine Veränderungen). Writings of the association for social politics, Bd. 132, 1910 (negotiations of the association in Vienna, 1909), P. 533-537.

11. --- The currency issue in a German-Austrian Customs Union (Die Währungsfrage bei einem deutſch-öſterreichiſchen Zollbündnis). Writings of the Association for Social Policy, Vol. 155, Part One, 1916, pp. 185-189.

II.
Essays from the Political Science Seminar (Staatswiſſenſchaftlichen Seminar) on Strasbourg i. E., edited by G. F. Knapp, Strasbourg, published by Karl Trübner:

Issue XII, 1894: Karl Helfferich, The consequences of the German-Austrian monetary union of 1857 (Die Folgen des deutſch-öſterreichiſchen Münzvereins von 1857), 134 S. -

Issue XV, 1895: Philipp Kalkmann, England's transition to the gold standard in the 18th century (Englands übergang zur Goldwährung im 18. Jahrhundert), 140 pp.

Issue XXIV, 1908: Kurt Blaum, The Money System of Switzerland since 1798 (Das Geldweſen der Schweiz ſeit 1798), 176 p.

Issue XXV, 1908: Johannes Scheffler, The United States of America in the 19th Century from the Viewpoint of the State (Das Geldweſen der Vereinigten Staaten von Amerika im 19. Jahrhundert vom Standpunkte des Staates), 123 pp.

Issue XXVI, 1910: Kurt Singer, The Motives of the Indian Monetary Reform (Die Motive der indiſchen Geldreform), 113 p.

Issue XXVII, 1911: Emil Frauz, The Constitution of Italian State Means of Payment since 1861 (Die Verfaſſung der ſtaatlichen Zahlungsmittel Italiens ſeit 1861), 174 pp.

Book XXVIII, 1912; Fritz Rühe, Spain's financial system since 1772 (Das Geldweſen Spaniens ſeit dem Jahre 1772), 304 p.

Issue XXX, 1913: Franz Gutmann, The French monetary system in the war (1870-1878) (Das franzöſiſche Geldweſen im Kriege (1870–1878)), 525 p.

Issue XXXI, 1914: Hermann Jllig, The Finance of France at the Time of the First Revolution to the End of the Paper Currency (Das Geldweſen Frankreichs zur Zeit der erſten Revolution bis zum Ende der Papierwährung), 87 p.

Issue XXXII, 1914: Alfred Schmidt, History of the English Monetary System in the 17th and 18th Centuries (Geſchichte des engliſchen Geldweſens im 17. und 18. Jahrhundert), 204 p.

Issue XXXIII, 1917: Johannes Wolter, The State Treasury of England at the Time of Bank Restriction (1797 to 1821) (Das ſtaatliche Geldweſen Englands zur Zeit der Bank-Reſtriktion (1797 bis 1821)), 214 p.

Issue XXXIV, 1918 (the last in the collection): Ludwig Bur, The revolution of the German economy in the war (Die Umwälzung der deutſchen Volkswirtſchaft im Kriege), 211 pages.

Outside this row is:
Erich Karl Mayer (from Mannheim), About the acceptance of banknotes at public coffers (über die Annahme von Banknoten an öffentlichen Kaſſen). Munich 1900. 28 S. Strasbourg doctoral dissertation.

The results of these investigations could not be incorporated into the later editions of the State Theory of Money without going beyond the narrow scope of the text: for the "Survey of States" is only one chapter and serves only to prove that the historical representation is inferior the new viewpoints is possible.

For future works on the history of finance, however, these works are extremely important; their authors would like to express their warmest thanks.

III. Judgments on the State Theory of Money.

S. P. Altmann, To the German money doctrine of the 19th century (Zur deutſchen Geldlehre des 19. Jahrhunderts); in: The Development of German Economics in the 19th Century, Leipzig 1908; P. 32 f. of the special imprint.

Maurice Ansiaux, La monnaie peut-elle être supprimée? in the Revue économique internationale, Bruxelles 1908, pp. 77-101; P. 85 f.

Friedrich Bendixen, The essence of money (Das Weſen des Geldes). Leipzig 1908, 60s .; The same, five-year monetary theory; in: Bank Archive, Volume X, 1911, No. 10; Pp. 145-148.

The same, Paper on Ludwig von Mises, theory of money and means of circulation (Referat über Ludwig von Miſes, Theorie des Geldes und der Umlaufsmittel); German literary newspaper 1912, No. 48; three columns about von Mises and the State Theory of Money. -

The same, Money and capital. Collected essays (Geld und Kapital. Geſammelte Auffätze). Leipzig 1912, 186 p. - Second Edition, Jena 1920.

The same, Review of the second edition of the State Theory of Money (Beſprechung der zweiten Auflage der Staatlichen Theorie des Geldes); in: Bank Archive, XVII. Vintage, No. 17 of June 1, 1918, p. 178.

The same, From theoretical metallism (criticism of the teachings of Karl Diehl) (Vom theoretiſchen Metallismus (Kritik der Lehren von Karl Diehl)) in the Jahrb. F. Nat.-Ök. u. Statistics, vol. 112 (3rd episode, vol. 57). Jena 1919, pp. 497-534.

The same, Monetary policy and theory of money in the light of the world war (Währungspolitik und Geldtheorie im Lichte des Weltkriegs). Munich and Leipzig 1916, 114 pp. Second edition, 1919.

L. von Bortkiewicz, The Monetary and Political Consequences of Nominalism (Die geldtheoretiſchen und währungspolitiſchen Konſequenzen des „Nominalismus"); in: Schmollers yearbook, Bd. XXX, 4th issue, 1906, pp. 1-34.

The same, The question of the reform of our currency and the Knapp's money theory (Die Frage der Reform unſerer Währung und die Knappiſche Geldtheorie); in: Annals for Social Policy and Legislation. (H. Braun), Vol. VI. Issue 1, 1918, pp. 57-102.

The same, Knapp's State Theory of Money (Knapps Staatliche Theorie des Geldes); in: the "Norddeutsche Allgemeine Zeitung" of 17 April 1918.

Ludwig Calligaris, State Theory of Money (Staatliche Theorie des Geldes); Article in the Munich "Allgemeine Zeitung" of 1 February 1906;

This is the first approving meeting. By the same author an article with the same heading in the Austrian Rundschau, Volume VII, Issue 80 of May 10, 1906. Also an article "The nature of money" in the journal "present" of April 13, 1907.

The same, Helfferich about Knapp (Helfferich über Knapp); in the Bank-Archiv, X. Volume, No. 17, 1911, pp. 268-270.

Karl Diehl, A New Theory of Money (Eine neue Theorie des Geldes); in: Bank Archive, 5th year, 1906, No. 21; the special imprint has 20 p. in 8°.

Karl Diehl, The Significance of Scientific Economics, etc. (Die Bedeutung der wiſſenſchaftlichen Nationalökonomie): Yearbooks of Economics and Statistics, Third Series, Vol. XXXVII, 1909, pp. 289-315; P. 310.

The same, About issues of monetary and currency (über Fragen des Geldweſens und der Valuta). Jena 1918, 140 p.

Karl Elster, For the analysis of the money problem; in the Yearbooks of Economics and Statistics (Zur Analyſe des Geldproblems; in den Jahrbüchern für Nationalökonomie und Statiſtik), 3rd Series, Vol. 54, 1917, pp. 257-303; especially p. 301.

The same, About the second edition of the State Theory of Money; in the annals of the national economy and statistics (Über die zweite Auflage der Staatlichen Theorie des Geldes), 3rd consequence, Bd. 56, 1918. S. 80-93.

The same, The current state of monetary theory and monetary policy problems (Zum heutigen Stande der geldtheoretiſchen und währungspolitiſchen Probleme), in: economy and administration, in Reich, state and commune, 1st year, Berlin 1920.

The same, The soul of money (Die Seele des Geldes). Jena 1920. 370 p.

Walther Federn, Modern Theory of Money in Austrian Bank Privileges (Moderne Geldtheorie im öfterreichifchen Bankprivilegium); in: Schmollers year book, Bd. XXXV 3rd book, 1911, P. 343-363; discusses the influence of the state theory of money on legislation in Austria-Hungary. Compare also: New Free Press, December 1, 1910, p. 3 below, the speech of Bilinski.

The same, To the renewal of bank privileges (Zur Erneuerung des Bankprivilegiums); in: Mit-Än der Industriellen Vereinigung, 1911, No. 4 (Vienna), p. 38.

The same, The Austrian economist: the article series "Metallist and state money theory" (Der öfterreichifche Volkswirt: die Artikelfolge „Metallift und ftaatliche Geldtheorie") in the 6th year, 1914, No. 36-41; and the article series "War and Money" in the 9th year, 1917, No. 36-50 and 10th year, 1917, No. 1.

Traugott Geering, A New Orientation of Currency Theory (Eine neue Orientierung der Währungstheorie); in the Neue Züricher Zeitung of May 10, 1907, First Evening. 4 columns.

The same, The latest phase in the theory of currency issues (Die neuefte Phafe in der Theorie der Währungsfrage); in the Basler Nachrichten, May 16, 1907. 2 columns.

Werner Genzmer, Critical Considerations on the Nominalist Money Theory (Kritifche Betrachtungen zur nominaliftifchen Geldtheorie). Freiburg doctoral dissertation, 1917, 94 p.

Paul Gerngroß, Contributions to an Economic Theory of Money (Beiträge zu einer wirtfchaftlichen Theorie des Geldes). Vienna and Leipzig, 1913, 37 p. (On Knapp and Bendixen).

Eberhard Gothein, War and economy (Krieg und Wirtfchaft). Academic speech. Heidelberg, 1914, 110 pages in 49; P. 82.

Ignaz Ritter Gruber of Menninger, On currency statistics (Zur Währungs-Statiſtik); in the Statistical Monatshefte, ed. from the k. k. Central Statistical Commission, new episode, XVIII. Vintage, Brno, 1913, p. 428-491, Appendix VI, note on the State Theory of Money.

Hakushi Tokuzo Fukuda, The Chartaltheorie as a new monetary theory. (Die Chartaltheorie als eine neue Geldtheorie) Handwritten German translation, 11 folio pages, from the year 1906, November issue of the Japanese magazine: Nihon Hagaku Shimpo.

Karl Helfferich, The money (Das Geld). Leipzig by C.L. Hirschfeld, second edition, 1910, 600 pp .; Foreword. (The first edition was published in 1903, ie before the State Theory of Money, even earlier are his works: History of the German monetary reform, Leipzig 1898, and contributions to the history of the German monetary reform, Leipzig 1898.
Helfferich was a beginner my student in Strasbourg. He may have had some advantage from my greater experience, but through him I have learned much from practice. His and Kalkmann's studies have led me to the State theory.)

Otto Heyn, On the question of the elimination of the value problem from the theory of money (Zur Frage der Eliminierung des Wertproblems aus der Geldtheorie); in: Journal of Social Science (by J. Wolf), new episode, Vol. IV, 1913, pp. 29-39. There, p. 29, the following sentence is written: "Among those who do not eliminate the problem of value, I too belong, and that is probably the only point in which mine, in 1894 (in the document: paper currency with gold reserve for foreign traffic) established monetary theory is different from Knapp's. "
Heyn's writing of 1894 (80 pages) is gratefully mentioned in the preface to the first edition of the State Theory of Money. The state theory puts their goals a little further.

Walter Hohenstein, The Essence of Money (Das Weſen des Geldes); in: The Bank, edited by Alfred Lansburgh, 3rd Issue, March 1908. 3 p.

Fritz Huber, Monetary theory and banking constitution (Geldtheorie und Bankverfaſſung); in: Bank Archive, XVI. Vintage, 1917, no. 15; Pp. 275-284.

Rudolf Keller, The end of the gold standard? (Das Ende der Goldwährung?) Prague, 1908, 36 p.; P. 5f.

Wilhelm König, Cash payment and bank separation (Barzahlung und Banktrennung). Vienna, 1907, 16 p.

Wilhelm König, Sidelights to the theory of the banknote (Streiflichter zur Theorie der Banknote). Vienna, 1909, 27 p. P. 16 f.

Leopold Kovács, The Independence of Banknotes from Gold (Die Unabhängigkeit des Banknotenumlaufes vom Golde). Graz, 1916; 78 p.

Ladon, Gold, silver, paper (Gold, Silber, Papier); in: "The Future", XV. Vintage, 1907, No. 27, pp. 35-38; P. 38.

A. Lansburgh, On Money (Vom Gelde); in: "The Bank", monthly published by Alfred Lansburgh, 11th issue, November 1910, pp. 1032-1038; is about the works of Knapp and Helfferich.

W. Lexis, A New Money Theory (Eine neue Geldtheorie); in: Archiv für Sozialwiſſenſchaft und Sozialpolitik, Vol. V, 1906, pp. 557-574.

W. Lexis, The Knapp's theory of money (Die Knappſche Geldtheorie); in: Yearbooks of Economics and Statistics, Third Series, Vol. XXXII, 1906, pp. 534-545.

Robert Liefmann, Money and gold. Economic theory of money (Geld und Gold. Ökonomiſche Theorie des Geldes). Stuttgart and Berlin, 1916, 241 pp .; Pp. 19, 117, 120, 162 and more often. -

Achille Loria, Statolatria monetaria; in: Riforma sociale, fasc. 8, anno XIII, volume XVI - seconda serie. Torino, 1906; 8 p. Statolatria is supposed to mean overestimation of the state.

Walther Lotz, G. F. Knapp's New Money Theory (G. F. Knapps neue Geldtheorie); in: Schmollers yearbook, Bd. XXX 2nd book, pp. 357-373 and Bd. XXX 1906, 3rd book, pp. 331-370.

Menadier, in the Journal of Numismatics, 1907, pp. 200-206 under "Literature": A review of the State Theory of Money (eine Befprechung der Staatlichen Theorie des Geldes).

Ludwig von Mises, Theory of money and means of circulation (Theorie des Geldes und der Umlaufsmittel). Munich and Leipzig, 1912; 476 p.

The same, For the classification of the money theories (Zur Klaffifikation der Geldtheorien), in the archive for social science (E. Jaffé) Bd. 44, booklet 1. 1917. P. 198-213.

Bruno Moll, Logic of money (Logik des Geldes). Munich and Leipzig, 1916; 104 p.

Wilhelm Müller (official of the Hungarian Communal Bank in Buda-Pest), The question of cash payment in the light of Knapp's theory of money (Die Frage der Barzahlung im Lichte der Knappfchen Geldtheorie). Vienna, 1908; 46 p. (Edited according to the Hungarian original).

Eugen Nübling, Coin or paper? An answer to G. F. Knapp's book on the state theory of money (Hartgeld oder Papier? Eine Antwort auf G. F. Knapps Buch über die ftaatliche Theorie des Geldes). Ulm, 1907; 55 p.

Melchior Palyi, Basic Problems of State Money Theory (Grundprobleme der ftaatlichen Geldtheorie), in: European State and Business Newspaper, Aug. 3, 1918.

Joh. Scheffler, State theory and pragmatic treatment of money (Staatliche Theorie und pragmatifche Behandlung des Geldes); in:

German Reichsbank sheets, 4th year 8th issue, pp. 145-152; 9th book, pp. 164-172; 10th issue, pp. 184-191; 11th issue, pp. 204-207, all Leipzig, 1906.

Alfred Schmidt (from Essen), Dr. Schwarzwald and the State Theory of Money (Dr. Schwarzwald und die Staatliche Theorie des Geldes); in: Bank Archive, XIII. Vintage No. 18 (1914), pp. 307-308.

The same, Recent Judgments on the State Theory of Money (Neuere Urteile über die Staatliche Theorie des Geldes); in: Schmollers year book, Bd. XLI 2nd book, 1917, S. 375-394; also numerous articles in the "Rheinisch-Westfälische Zeitung".

The same, Knapp's school and the younger money theorists (Knapps Schule und die jüngeren Geldtheoretiker); in: North German General newspaper of 15 May 1918; in the economic part, 3 columns.

Alfred Schmidt (from Essen), The State Theory of Money (Die Staatliche Theorie des Geldes); in the European State and Economic Newspaper of July 20, 1918, p. 537.

The same, The State Monetary Policy in the System of Chartal Theory (Die ſtaatliche Währungspolitik im Syſtem der Chartal-theorie), in the World Economic Archives, Vol. XVI, Number 1 u. 2, July and October 1920.

F. Frh. Von Schrötter, Knapp's Chartalismus (Knapps Chartalismus); in: "Berliner Münzblätter", new episode, XXVIII. Vintage No. 63, March 1907, p. 473-502.

Hermann Schumacher, The German Monetary System and its Reform (Die deutſche Geldverfaſſung und ihre Reform); in: Schmollers Yearbook, Bd. XXXII Issue 4, 1908, pp. 1-132; P. 1.

Hermann Schwarzwald, Gold currency without gold (Goldwährung ohne Gold); in: Bank Archive, XIII. Year No. 16, May 15, 1914, pp. 268-273;

especially p. 272 f.

Kurt Singer, The War and the Money Problem (Der Krieg und das Geldproblem) (Lecture, held in Hamburg on March 28, 1917); in: Publications of the German Business Association for South and Central America, Issue 1, Berlin, 1917, pp. 86-104. - Summarizes the views of Knapp and Bendixen shortly.

The same, The State Theory of Money (Die Staatliche Theorie des Geldes), in: Economic Service, No. 13, of March 29, 1918. 2 pp. -

The same, The money as a sign (Das Geld als Zeichen). Jena 1920. 206 p.

Kiichiro Soda, The New Knapp's Money Theory and the Essence of Money (Die neue Knappſche Geldtheorie und das Weſen des Geldes); Yearbooks of National Economy and Statistics, Third Series, Vol. XXXIV, 1907, pp. 336-355 and pp. 620-655.

The same, Money and value (Geld und Wert). Tübingen, 1909, 176 pp.; P. 37f. Paul Steller, State Theory of Money; in: "Berliner Aktionär" of June 14, 1916; 2 p.

The same, Logic of money (Logik des Geldes); in: "Berliner Aktionär" of July 1, 1916; short note about Knapp and Bruno minor.

Ludwig Stephinger, Economic Theory of Money (Volkswirtſchaftliche Theorie des Geldes); in the magazine for the entire political science, 1911, P. 114 to 132.

Miklos Ungar, Monetary theory and currency (Geldtheorie und Valuta); in: Schoenberger's Börsenund Handelsbericht, Vienna, September 10, 1916. The author lived in Budapest; he died.

Andreas Voigt, The State Theory of Money (Die ſtaatliche Theorie des Geldes); in: Time-Ä for the entire political science, 62nd year, 1906 ,.

317-340.

The same, Theory of monetary transactions (Theorie des Geldverkehrs). Journal of Social Science, founded by J. Wolf, Neue Folge, XI. Vintage, 1920, Issue 5 and 6. -

Adolf Wagner, Theoretical Social Economics (Theoretifche Sozialökonomik), second section, second volume: Socioeconomic Theory of Money and Money. Leipzig. 1909, pp. 111-799; especially pages 112, 115, 157, 600, 729 (see above the discussion of J.W.

Knut Wicksell, Knapp's pennigteori; in: Särtryck Ekonomisk Tidskrift, 1907, p. 41-52.

Friedrich Frhr. von Wieser, Theory of Social Economy (Theorie der gefellfchaftlichen Wirtfchaft); in: Grundriß der Sozialökonomik, I. Department, Tübingen, 1914, p. 321.

J. W., Review of Adolph Wagner's Theoretical Socioeconomics of 1909 (Befprechung von Adolph Wagners Theoretifcher Sozialökonomik vom Jahre 1909); in Julius Wolf's Zeitschrift für Sozialwissenschaft, XII. Vintage, 1909, pp. 758-760; P. 759.

Martin Wolff, The money (Das Geld). 90 pages in Ehrenberg's Handbook of Commercial Law, IV. Vol., 1st Division, 1917.

Otto von Zwiedineck, The Income as a monetary value determination reason (Die Einkommensgeftaltung als Geldwertbeftimmungsgrund); Schmollers Yearbook, Vol. XXXIII, 1917, pp. 131-189; P. 134.

(Anonymous), Against metallism (Gegen den Metallismus). Article in the "New Hamburg Stock Exchange" of June 10, 1914 (about Knapp and Dr. Schwarzwald).

The mentioned writings, ordered by time:

1906. von Bortkiewicz. Calligaris. Diehl. Hakushi. Lexis. Loria. Lotz. Scheffler. Voigt.
1907. Calligaris. Geering. König. Ladon. Menadier. Nübling. von Schrötter. Soda. Wickſell.
1908. Altmann. Anſiaux. Bendixen. Hohenſtein. Keller. Wilhelm Müller. Schumacher.
1909. Diehl. König. Soda. A. Wagner. J. W.
1910. Helfferich. Lansburgh.
1911. Bendixen. Calligaris. Federn. Stephinger.
1912. Bendixen. von Miſes.
1913. Gerngroß. Gruber von Menninger. Heyn.
1914. Federn. Gothein. Alfred Schmidt-Eſſen. Schwarzwald. von Wieſer.
1915. fehlt.
1916. Bendixen. Kovács. Liefmann. Moll. Steller. Ungar.
1917. K. Elſter. Federn. Huber. Genzmer. von Miſes. Alfred Schmidt-Eſſen. Singer. von Zwiedineck.
1918. Bendixen. von Bortkiewicz. Diehl. K. Elſter. Palyi. Alfred Schmidt-Eſſen. Singer.
1919. Bendixen.
1920. Bendixen. K. Elſter. Alfred Schmidt-Eſſen. Singer. Voigt.
1921. K. Elſter. Kerſchagl. Alfred Schmidt-Eſſen. Max Weber.
1917. K. Elster. Feathers. Huber. Genzmer. from Mises. Alfred Schmidt-Essen. Singer. from Zwiedineck.
1918. Bendixen. from Bortkiewicz. Diehl. K. magpie. Palyi. Alfred Schmidt-Essen. Singer.
1919. Bendixen.
1920. Bendixen. K. magpie. Alfred Schmidt-Essen. Singer. Voigt.
1921. K. Elster. Kerschagl. Alfred Schmidt-Essen. Max Weber.

Postscript (on page 450 ff.).

By Karl Elster has still appeared: German misery in the light of currency theory. Collected essays, Jena 1921, 124 pages.

From Austria is available: Dr. med. Richard Kerschagl, The Doctrine of Money in the Economy. Universalism and individualism. Vienna 1921, 60 pages.

Max Weber has pronounced himself so stormy in the State Theory of Money that modesty forbids me to repeat his words; see. Outline of Social Economics, III. Department, Economy and Society, First Part, Tübingen 1921, page 99, 105, 109-113.

Darmstadt, February 26, 1921.
G. F. Knapp.

www.ingramcontent.com/pod-product-compliance
Lightning Source LLC
Chambersburg PA
CBHW031625210526
45464CB00004B/1745